The Backyard Homestead Manual

A How-To Guide to Homesteading-Self Sufficient Urban Farming Made Easy

CHASE BOURN

Contents

INTRODUCTION

"The greatest fine art of the future will
be the making of a comfortable living
from a small piece of land."

-Abraham Lincoln

ONE OF THE greatest joys in life is to plan, grow,
and harvest your own bountiful food supply.
Homesteading can have many meanings.
Most commonly, it refers to someone who is living off
of the land, utilizing the food that they grow and raise.

There is a big problem with today's modern food
production. Everything is over-processed and filled
with sugar and other crazy ingredients that you can't
pronounce, much less know where they come from.

Many people have grown tired of modern food
production methods that are only making them sicker
and sicker. They are longing for a solution to producing
healthy and sustainable food. That solution is known as
homesteading.

While many people dream of owning their own little slice of heaven by homesteading, there is a lot to consider before getting started.

Wouldn't it be great if there was a step-by-step guide that showed you exactly what you need to do in order to set up a successful homestead from the beginning? That is exactly what this book is all about!

This book will serve as your complete guide to everything you need to know in order to start a successful homestead and make your self-sufficient, urban farming dreams come true. I am going to outline everything you need to know, from the legalese of zoning and regulations to how to make money from your bounty, and everything in between.

But before we get started, I want to introduce myself.

My name is Chase Bourn. I have lived as a backyard homesteader for over five years on 2 acres of land that I own. For over seven years, I have been living my dream of self-reliance through a very minimalistic and eco-friendly lifestyle, completely off the grid. During this time, I have made a lot of mistakes and gained a lot of knowledge that I now want to share with you.

When you decide to start your homestead, there is a lot you will need to learn. It is my goal to be able to share my knowledge with you so that you can set yourself up for success right from the beginning, avoiding some of the costly mistakes that I myself have made.

When I lived in the city, I used to dream of being a homesteader. It is a lot of hard work but it is worth every second. Every day, I am working on my farm or with my animals, providing for myself and my family. I relish in the beauty of creating something from scratch and knowing that what I am doing is adding to the Earth rather than taking away from it. Every day I wake up and get to live my dream of owning a homestead where I am self-sustaining myself and my family with my urban farm, and I couldn't be happier.

Over the last few years, I have worked with dozens of people to help them successfully make the transition to homestead living. It is my hope in writing this book that I am able to help thousands of more people successfully transition into their own homesteads. It feels great when I get snail mail and emails from people that are using my knowledge to build their dreams.

I am going to make you a promise with this book.

If you read this book cover to cover you will be ready to start your own homestead in no time. Even if you have never successfully grown a vegetable in your life or handled livestock, this book will show you how to become a homesteader. I am going to arm you with the knowledge you need, you just have to add the desire and motivation to get things moving.

So what are you waiting for?

If you truly want to be a homesteader, then stop putting it off. Stop making excuses and stop saying *"Someday I'll do it"*. Start putting that someday plan into action now. Don't look back on your dreams with regret and wish about all of the things that you should have done. Do your research, make a plan, and put that plan into action.

The Backyard Homestead Manual will take you by the hand and show you step-by-step everything that you need to start living your dream homestead life. I cannot emphasize enough the joy and satisfaction that I experience every day, living my sustainable urban farming lifestyle. It is truly an amazing way to live and it's all outlined for you in this book.

You might already be asking these questions:

- *What can and can't I do on a homestead?*
- *What will I need to get started?*
- *What will I grow or raise?*

Don't worry; I will cover all of that and more for you in great depth in this book.

Here is just a small sample of the topics that I will cover:

- The laws, regulations, zoning, and permits required for activities and structures on your homestead.
- The tools and gear that you will need to be successful.
- The growing seasons in different areas across the United States.
- Necessary elements for quality soil.
- How to design and map out your growing spaces.

- ☒ How to spot potential issues with your farming.
- ☒ Which farm records you should be keeping.
- ☒ How to prepare your ground for planting.
- ☒ Using raised beds, container gardening, and planting directly into the ground.
- ☒ How to germinate plants indoors.
- ☒ All about crop rotation and succession planting.
- ☒ Pests and disease prevention for your plants.
- ☒ How and when to harvest your bounty.
- ☒ Activities to do in the fall to keep your farm running smoothly.
- ☒ The 13 different categories of plants and what you need to know about each one.
- ☒ How to preserve and store your food.
- ☒ How to can, dry, freeze, ferment, cold store, and seed save.
- ☒ How to raise animals for production and butchering.
- ☒ How to profit from the products you are producing from your land.

Keep reading and you will become a master self-sufficient, urban farming homesteader, in no time.

And then make sure to share this book with anyone that you know that is interested in homesteading or gardening (there is a lot of good info on that as well)!

CHAPTER ONE
Requirements, Resources, and Constraints

I T TRULY TAKES a lot to get a homestead started, particularly in regard to the tools, gear, and equipment that you will need. You should also be aware of any local zoning laws and regulations required for carrying out tasks on your property. Homestead properties generally require more storage than traditional houses. Advanced planning for electrical lines and watering systems also need to be put into place. Additionally, homesteaders need to be knowledgeable of the growing season, growth rate factors, the elevation of their land, and availability of water resources.

In this chapter, we are going to cover all of the different requirements and resources needed as well as potential constraints that homesteaders face.

Legal: Laws and Regulations

Before you start digging up land and building, you should be aware of all laws and regulations in your specific area. Declaring your property as a homestead through an official "Declaration of Homestead" document can help to protect your property and home against creditors in an economic hardship.

Homesteads were much more prevalent in the days of pioneers. Spread throughout the United States, homesteaders were self-sufficient, growing their own food, and even making their own clothes using the resources available on their properties. Many people are turning to modernized homesteads as a way to get back to their roots and break the routines of urban living. While modern homesteading is much more convenient than in the pioneer days, you need to make sure that you research your local laws and regulations. Ideally, this should be done before purchasing a property.

The most basic zoning regulations include residential and commercial zoning. Residential zoning is meant for individual living accommodations. Properties that are zoned as commercial are meant to be used to provide services or produce goods that are sold. Zoning regulations can be complicated especially when considering homestead properties. If your property is zoned as residential then you may be prohibited from legally keeping livestock on the premises. This can also regulate the number of certain animals you can keep per acre. And if animals and livestock are allowed on the property, it might come with certain restrictions.

It is advised that you contact your local zoning department directly. Don't rely on simply reading zoning information. Instead, clarify any questions you might have with someone from the department. If necessary, contact the zoning department multiple times and speak with different individuals while asking the same questions. This will ensure that you get a consistent answer every time.

Make sure that you are documenting all of the information regarding your property. Take note of when you spoke to the zoning department and what information was communicated to you. This way, if there is ever any legal action taken against you in regard to zoning, you have proof of the information you received.

You might also require different permits depending on what types of activities you are planning to do on your homestead. For example, some areas require permits for beekeeping while others do not. Also, if you are planning on putting up any additional structures or adding to any buildings then check with your local zoning department for any required building permits.

Utility lines

Make sure that whenever you are digging in the ground you check for utility lines. You can do this by contacting your local utility company, even if you are currently not connected to the utility lines. Digging in an area without knowing if there are any utility lines can be very dangerous and potentially very expensive. Avoid this headache by doing a little bit of leg work first.

Tools, Gear, and Equipment

You are going to need a lot of tools, gear, and equipment to get your homestead started. When possible, purchase used items to save on your initial costs. You don't have to worry about buying everything you are going to need right off the bat. You can start with the bare minimum and add more tools and equipment as you continue to grow your homestead. Certain equipment can also be rented if you are not using it consistently.

Basic tools

Your most basic tools are going to be common items that you would have in a toolbox or workshop and will include the following:

- ☒ A hammer and other hand tools
- ☒ A drill
- ☒ A sawmill
- ☒ Pliers
- ☒ Nails and screws
- ☒ A staple gun
- ☒ Wrenches
- ☒ Safety equipment (gloves, masks)

While not essential, a tractor, ATV, or other farming vehicle is also helpful for hauling things and moving heavier items around.

Gardening tools, such as shovels and rakes, are also essential for preparing your crops. You will also need ladders, hoses, and very long extension cords. You will realize that the more projects you do around your homestead, the more tools and equipment you will need. However, there is nothing wrong with starting out with just the basics and adding on as you go.

Storage

Of course, with a homestead, you are going to need various outdoor storage areas. These can be for storing tools, equipment, vehicles and even livestock. If the homestead already has existing storage structures in place then you can work to maximize the space used within those structures. If there are not enough storage areas then you can always build more or purchase pre-built structures.

Many storage structures are simple to build and can even be done in a weekend. Four walls, a roof, and a locking door are all you really need for a basic storage unit. You can add things like workshop areas, a floor, and even heat if you want to use the area as a workshop in addition to storage.

Watering systems

We discuss farming irrigation systems in much more depth in chapter three. Watering systems can be simple or complex. If you have smaller plots, then simply use a hose with holes punched in it and place it at the base of your plants. Then you will only need to turn on the hose periodically in order to provide the plants with water. Or you can have a larger irrigation system that includes timers and covers a much larger area. This will depend on how many planting plots you have.

Electrical lines

Before you start digging, you are going to need to contact your local utility company in order to determine if there are any electrical lines in the area. If you are taking on a larger project, such as creating new gardening plots over several acres, then you can get someone from the utility company to come out and survey your property and mark where any utility lines are. This will ensure that you are safely digging.

The Growing Season

The length of your growing season is going to depend on the area in which you live and its climate. North America is divided into several planting or hardiness zones. You should familiarize yourself with your hardiness zone in order to properly plan your crops.

The hardiness zones are as follows:

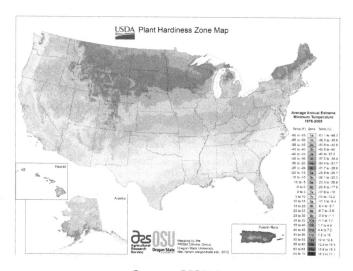

USDA Plant Hardiness Zone Map

Source: USDA

The main purpose of the USDA growing zone map is to represent the minimum average winter temperatures within that region. However, there are other factors that can contribute to the success or failure of your crops. While the map can provide you with a lot of good information, it is not perfect and does not account for things like snow cover or freezing and thawing cycles. You can use the hardiness zone map by first figuring out which zone you are in. Almost every state has different zones. The growing zones also focus on the adoption of permanent landscape plants, such as trees, shrubs, or perennials, and not necessarily garden variety crops. Updated maps specific to each state and region can be found on the USDA website.

Crop Growth Rate Factors

There are four main factors that affect the rate of plant growth: water, temperature, light, and nutrients. More or less of any one of these can affect how quickly or how slowly a plant grows. You should be knowledgeable about each one of these factors so that you can give your plants the best possible conditions for successful growing.

You should understand the types and kinds of lights that your plants will need before planting them. From season to season lighting can also vary in intensity. Come spring, the intensity of the natural light increases and brings the plants out of dormancy. The summer sunlight encourages flowering and fruiting on trees and plants, as well as the growth of vegetables. In the fall, the decreasing light causes the leaves to change color and fall.

Plants need water to survive, and many of them need a lot. A plant is about 90% water and without it becomes easily stressed and dies. Water keeps the plant hydrated and nourished, while also helping to deliver nutrients to the soil. The roots of the plant also help to absorb nutrients from the soil after watering. While many plants thrive on a lot of water, overwatering a plant can also kill it. This is why it is important to know the right amount of water for your crops.

14

The environmental temperature also affects the life processes of the plants by speeding them up or slowing them down. Warmer weather helps to speed up the germination and growing process. Warmer temperatures speed up the photosynthesis process which helps the plants to grow quicker. During cooler temperatures, the growing slows down. While crops can still grow during the winter months, it will take longer for them to fully mature.

There are exactly 17 nutrients that plants need to survive. All of them except for oxygen, hydrogen, and carbon, are not naturally occurring in air and water. If any of these 17 nutrients are lacking, the plant is not able to thrive and growth will be stunted.

The nutrients found within the soil are divided into micronutrients and macronutrients, just like with essential human nutrients. However, unlike the macronutrients that humans need (carbohydrates, fats, and proteins) the macronutrients that plants need include nitrogen, calcium, sulfur, potassium, magnesium, and phosphorus. The micronutrients are elemental and include iron and copper. In order to get the best possible crops, you should be providing your soil with all 17 nutrients.

Adding nutrients is not the same thing as adding fertilizers. Many fertilizers only include nitrogen, phosphorus, and potassium but none of the other essential nutrients. You can avoid plant diseases by adding essential nutrients to the soil amendments.

The 17 essential plant nutrients include:

- ☒ Nitrogen
- ☒ Phosphorus
- ☒ Potassium
- ☒ Calcium
- ☒ Magnesium
- ☒ Sulfur
- ☒ Chlorine
- ☒ Iron
- ☒ Manganese
- ☒ Zinc
- ☒ Copper
- ☒ Boron
- ☒ Molybdenum
- ☒ Nickel
- ☒ Oxygen
- ☒ Carbon
- ☒ Hydrogen

Just like humans, plants need a diet with balanced nutrients to thrive and cannot live off of junk food.

Available Planting Space

When you are planning out your crops and plots, you will have to determine your overall available space. You will also have to factor in any necessary space for animals and livestock. You can really maximize the area available on your land when you plan in advance. The different kinds of planting methods you are using (container planting, raised beds, or planting directly into the ground) will be a very large factor in how much room you need for your crops. The different types of crops you are planting will also be a deciding factor on how much space you will need.

If you are including animals in your homestead, you will most likely need pasture for them to graze. Obviously, the larger the animal, the more pasture space you will need. You will also need to determine the purpose of your homestead before moving into the space planning process. Are you going to be growing and producing just to satisfy the needs of your family or are you doing it as a means to make an income for your family? If you are going to be growing and producing to sell, you are going to need to consider the amount of space you will need. For example, you only need about six chickens to produce eggs for a family. However, you will need a lot more chickens, therefore a lot more space, in order to produce eggs to sell.

Elevation and Drainage

The elevation of your property, and the ability for water to drain, can drastically affect the health of your crops. These two factors come into play when planning out what you are going to plant and where. If you have a sloping terrain, water runoff can become a large problem. You will want to avoid planting crops in areas of lower elevation to avoid flooding. The elevation of your property can also affect your crops due to changes in weather. For example, homesteads in higher elevations tend to get colder more quickly.

Availability of Water

Water can come from various sources. One of the best ways to get the water you need to provide for your crops is to use rain barrels. This can easily be done by purchasing 55-gallon drums which can be placed under the downspouts of houses or other outdoor structures. The rain then runs off into the downspouts and into the rain barrels, collecting rainwater to use around the homestead.

Chapter Summary

A lot of planning goes into starting a homestead. Before purchasing land or digging up your property, you will need to ensure that you are aware of the laws and regulations in your specific area. You want to make sure that you are not digging into any utility lines, are obtaining the proper permits when necessary, and you are coordinating with all zoning regulations.

Starting a homestead also requires a lot of tools and equipment. Some of the most basic things you will need to get started are hand tools and anything else that you would normally find at home. Some of the more homestead specific equipment includes things like an ATV, tractor, or other large vehicles to help haul heavier items. Of course, you cannot forget about essential gardening tools and very long extension cords. You must also make sure that you have enough room to store your tools and equipment.

When planning out the crops that you want to grow on your homestead, you should familiarize yourself with the hardiness zone that you are in and what kind of crops work best in that zone.

Your crops will need four main things to be successful: water, the right temperature, light, and nutrients. Having more or less of any one of these factors can result in lower yields. You should also make sure that your plants are getting all 17 of their essential nutrients to thrive. What and how much you decide to plant will greatly depend on your available planting space, as well as the kinds of planting methods you use. You must also calculate the amount of land necessary for any livestock that will need pasture to graze.

Other important factors to consider when planning your homestead are: elevation, water drainage, and the availability of water. You will want to avoid planting your crops where water runoff can become a problem. Furthermore, you can save rain water to help provide water for your crops.

CHAPTER TWO
Planning Your Homestead

P LANNING YOUR HOMESTEAD is extremely important. You can't just go around your property and start to dig things up and think that you are going to be successful by doing this. Planning out your homestead is so important for several reasons.

First, a plan helps you determine the best use of your property and won't leave your land under or over utilized. You need to determine what type of plants you are going to have and where they will be placed. You don't want to go planting a bunch of random vegetables that you are not going to eat because you don't like them. Plant things that you know you like and that you and your family are going to use.

Planning also helps you to be more efficient and effective. Poor planning can lead to wasted time and resources. Wasting time and resources due to poor planning is completely preventable.

Develop a Planting Plan

Before you go out and start to buy seeds or soil, you need to plan out exactly what you are going to plant. More specifically, you need to plan the types of plants that you are going to plant, and the amount of each. There are many free garden planners online that you can access to help plan out your garden.

Sit down, either by yourself or with your family, and determine which types of fruits and vegetables you would like to grow on your farm. If you are totally new to gardening and farming like I was then this might take some trial and error. While you can grow many different things throughout the various growing zones across the United States (more on this in a later chapter), some of the things that you want to grow might not do very well in certain areas.

When you are putting together your initial plan here are a couple of things to consider:

- ☒ How much space you have to use.
- ☒ What you and your family are going to eat.
- ☒ How much food you need to be producing to feed your family.
- ☒ Your planting schedule.
- ☒ Any potential issues that could arise.
- ☒ When you will be harvesting.
- ☒ How you plan to preserve your food.

Take a deep dive into the different types of plants you are going to want to eat, and therefore, plant. Then you should cross-reference if those plants are ideal for your area. For example, while I love eating bananas, there are not many ideal locations within the United States for growing bananas.

There are also many foods that you might not have previously considered growing that might do very well in your area. For example, you can easily grow grains, which can be used for both human consumption and livestock feed.

Types of things to plant and grow

What you determine to plant and grow is going to drastically depend on your homestead location. Some of the more common products to grow include root vegetables, Brassicas, leafy greens, legumes, nightshades, and vine crops. You can also grow a wide variety of fruits, such as fruit-bearing trees and bushes.

Root vegetables include anything that grows in the ground, such as:

- ☒ Beets
- ☒ Carrots
- ☒ Turnips
- ☒ Radishes
- ☒ Parsnips
- ☒ Rutabagas
- ☒ Onions
- ☒ Garlic
- ☒ Sweet potatoes
- ☒ Leeks

Brassicas are those vegetables that are related to the cabbage, such as:

- ☒ Cabbage
- ☒ Kale
- ☒ Broccoli
- ☒ Collards
- ☒ Cauliflower
- ☒ Kohlrabi
- ☒ Brussels sprouts

Leafy greens can often be confused with Brassicas, but are leafier. These include:

- ☒ Spinach
- ☒ Lettuce
- ☒ Chard
- ☒ Watercress
- ☒ Microgreens
- ☒ Sprouts
- ☒ Arugula
- ☒ Endive
- ☒ Bok choy
- ☒ Any of the green tops of root vegetables

Nightshades are actually a little confusing when it comes to their classification, as many of them, excluding potatoes, are technically fruits as they contain internal seeds. Nightshades include:

- ☒ Tomatoes
- ☒ Peppers

- ☒ Chilis
- ☒ Eggplant
- ☒ White potatoes
- ☒ Red potatoes

Legumes can often be confused with grains, but are a type of vegetable and include:

- ☒ Peas
- ☒ All types of beans
- ☒ Lima beans
- ☒ Lentils
- ☒ Peanuts
- ☒ Soybeans
- ☒ Chickpeas

Lastly, vine crops are actually more fruits than vegetables and need a lot of space to grow. Vine crops include:

- ☒ Melons
- ☒ Zucchini
- ☒ Cucumbers
- ☒ Squash
- ☒ Pumpkins
- ☒ Gourdes

Then there is corn, which has some debate as to what category to place it in. When field corn is harvested it is dry and considered a grain. When sweet corn is grown in a garden or homestead farm and harvested fresh, it is considered a vegetable. Although technically speaking, due to its biological makeup, it's actually a fruit. So technically speaking, it is a grain, a vegetable, and a fruit.

Mapping Out Your Space

As I previously mentioned, there are applications and websites online that you can use to plan out your garden, making it very easy to include all of the different types of plants that you want to grow on your homestead. Or, you can certainly do it the old fashioned way and draw out your property with a pen and paper to determine where you are going to put each type of plant.

During your planning process, you must also be aware of the yield you will likely get from each plant. You can use seed catalogs to help determine the estimated crop yield. Planning out what you are going to plant is also vital to proper spacing. If you aren't aware of how much space vine crops need, you will likely get an overgrowth and your yield will suffer. When you are drawing out your farm or garden, to get maximum sun exposure, focus on planting the tallest plants on the north side. This way, the tallest crops will not shade the smaller crops. Planting the various aforementioned vegetable families together in groups makes it easier to plan the planting rotation in future years. You can also get maximum sun exposure by running your planting rows north to south (more on this in chapter three).

If you have never done gardening before, I suggest

that you start small. Don't try and grow everything at once and don't try to grow things that are difficult. Stick to the easier crops and figure out some great recipes that you can make from easy to grow produce. Whatever you can't grow, you can always buy from the store or order it online as well.

Systematize Your Process

Whether you are running a business or running a farm, you should have a system for all of your processes. This is very helpful when you are first starting out. Figure out how to do a task, write it down and attach any resources, then keep that handy for the next time that you need to do the same thing.

In business, this system is called Standard Operating Procedures, or SOPs. You can create SOPs for just about any area of your life and urban farming is no different. When you are not doing something day in and day out, you might forget about some important steps. When you have everything systematized, you don't need to worry about forgetting any important steps and you can get consistent results time and time again. For example, perhaps one season you used a certain amount of fertilizer and you got the best tomatoes ever. This is where you would write things down and document them. That way, you know for the next growing season you are able to duplicate those results.

Having these processes in place also allows you to

be able to quickly identify different issues before they arise.

Record Keeping For Your Farm

Just as with having your processes systematized, you should also keep records of things that you do around your farm. This, again, will help you to get consistent results with your efforts.

Each season, you should record where you are placing certain plants, the actions you are taking with each of those plants, and the outcomes you are getting. Basically, a journal of your farming processes. Draw your crops out on a map to ensure that you are properly rotating them.

You can easily keep a record of what you have planted, the estimated yield, and when you should harvest the produce. Make a simple spreadsheet on your computer or in a planting notebook that looks similar to the table below.

Type of Plant	Date Planted	Estimated Yield	When to Harvest

Keeping an Effective Planting Schedule

Keeping an effective planting schedule comes down to plant phenology. Phenology is the study of the timing of biological events in plants and animals such as flowering, hibernation, reproduction, and migration. The study of phenology focuses on the timing of these events in relation to seasonal and climate changes.

Plant phenology

Much like plants and animals make changes based on seasonal cues, so can the urban farmer. The word phenology literally translates to "the science of appearance", which means that you as an urban farmer can use the appearance of environmental and seasonal cues to determine the next step in the farming process.

Using phenology, we can determine what to plant, when to plant, and where. You must also consider factoring in the days to maturity, or when you can harvest your bounty, which you can do with the help of a seed catalog. The time of harvest is greatly dependent on variations in temperatures throughout the different growing zones. It is best to choose disease-resistant plants, especially if you are not an expert gardener to begin with.

Some crops should be planted in early spring after the last frost hits as they are cold-tolerant plants, while others should be planted in the middle of the summer. Some crops will grow much quicker than others and will greatly depend on the variations in temperatures.

You can also use plant phenology by using indicator plants to determine when certain pests and insects will be active and when particular weather conditions will prevail. Here are a few tips according to plant phenology that will make your farming efforts more successful:

- ☒ When the daffodils bloom, plant your Swiss chard, spinach, beets, and onions.
- ☒ When the maple trees flower, plant your peas.
- ☒ When the leaves of the white oak trees are about the size of a cat ear, plant your potatoes.
- ☒ When the apple trees drop their petals, plant your bush beans, pole beans, and cucumbers.
- ☒ When peony bushes and black locust trees flower, it's time to transplant tomatoes, melons, and eggplants.

Additionally, you will want to transplant plants right before it rains so that all of your transplanted plants become well watered. You can tell when it's going to rain when Swallows start to swoop towards the ground in the fields. Swallows eat flying insects that tend to fly closer to the ground right before it rains.

Cold-season vegetables

The beginning of the cold season is indicated by night-time temperatures staying between 60 degrees Fahrenheit and 25 degrees Fahrenheit. Depending on the location, the cold weather season might last anywhere between 60 to 110 days. Staggered planting (described below) is good to practice in the cold weather months to ensure that you get a consistent supply of produce.

- ☒ Cold-season vegetables include:
- ☒ Arugula
- ☒ Beets
- ☒ Broad beans
- ☒ Broccoli
- ☒ Broccoli raab
- ☒ Brussel sprouts
- ☒ Cabbage
- ☒ Cauliflower
- ☒ Chinese cabbage
- ☒ Collards
- ☒ Corn salad
- ☒ Endive
- ☒ Florence fennel
- ☒ Kohlrabi
- ☒ Lettuce
- ☒ Parsley
- ☒ Parsnips
- ☒ Peas
- ☒ Radicchio
- ☒ Radishes
- ☒ Red mustard
- ☒ Spinach
- ☒ Turnips

Warm-season vegetables

When farmers start to plant their warm-season vegetables, it marks the transition from winter to summer and from gardening indoors to gardening outdoors. The in-ground soil will now be warm enough to grow everything. While some warm-season plants do well in both warm and cold weather, others will only thrive in warm weather.

Warm-season vegetables include:

- Artichokes
- Asparagus
- Bush beans
- Carrots
- Celery
- Corn (sweet and popcorn)
- Cucumbers
- Eggplants
- Garlic
- Leeks
- Muskmelons
- Okra
- Bulb onions
- Peanuts
- Sweet peppers
- Pole beans
- Potatoes
- Pumpkin
- Summer and winter squash
- Sweet potatoes
- Swiss chard
- Tomatoes
- Watermelons
- Rhubarb

Staggered planting

If you already have a solid harvesting and preservation plan in place, then you might not need to consider staggered planting. However, there are times when farmers and gardeners can get hit with way more food than they know what to do with. When you are planting all of your vegetable groups at once, it is likely that you will be harvesting them all at once too. While this is great if you are planning on selling your produce or have a very big family to feed, you might not want one hundred pounds of zucchini all at the same time (don't ask me how I know that).

Staggered planting allows you to sow a few seeds or plots every one to two weeks over the course of a month to extend your harvest and keep your crops coming in at a reasonable pace. Depending on the length of your growing season, you can stagger your planting for just about any crop. It's advised that you stagger crops that tend to mature all at once or don't preserve well, such as leafy greens.

Staggering your planting also helps fight against crops that are prone to pest and insect attacks. When you are able to stagger your planting and plant successive crops, you will have one harvest ripening when the pests and diseases are affecting the other crop. Specifically, melons are a good crop to stagger as it can be difficult to store many melons at once. Flowers can also benefit from staggered planting and they will keep your beautiful garden blooming all year long.

While the concept of staggered planting is very easy,

it can take some trial and error and careful calculation to get it right. Do your best to estimate how much food you would like to harvest in a given week and start your planting according to that. You will also have to consider the season's average growing temperature and estimate if the crops will mature enough to harvest at the point you would like them to. A general rule of thumb is to plant seeds for that specific crop every 10 to 28 days. Before you start sowing your seeds, be sure to check your regional maps for the best growing times for all of the crops that you would like to plant.

Here are a few examples of the number of days that you should stagger certain crops:

- Lettuce, onions, and peas: every 10 days
- Bush beans: every 14 to 21 days
- Radishes and turnips: every 10 to 14 days
- Melons: every 5 to 10 days

Planting intervals for various types of vegetables

7-Day	10-Day	14-Day	21-Day	30-Day
Baby leaf lettuce	Full-sized head lettuce	Beets	Carrots	Summer squash
Baby leaf greens	Full-sized Asian Greens & Bok Choy	Escarole	Cucumbers	Swiss chard
Radishes	Fresh-eating kohlrabi	Endive	Full-sized mustard greens	
Spinach	Peas	Arugula	Melons	
	Sweet corn	Turnips		
	Bush beans			

Longer growing seasons give you the ability to stagger the planting of your crops for longer periods of time. Depending on the weather, you can start staggering your planting at the very beginning of the growing season and extend right through to the end of the season. This will allow you to harvest your crops for significantly longer then if you were to plant everything at once.

When early spring comes and seeds become readily available, stock up! Before you start your staggered planting, prepare all of the plots that you are going to use. This will prevent disturbing the existing plants when you go to add new ones. You can also help to speed up the planting process by germinating the seeds in advance and by planting an already existing plant rather than starting from a seed. Some plants offer early-ripening varieties which can also help to speed up the harvest. Try experimenting with some of these, but remember to take notes!

Succession planting

Succession planting is very similar to staggered planting in that you space out the planting of the same type of crop every few days to every few weeks. This helps to prevent the feast or famine that generally happens when everything is planted at once. This way, you will continually have new crops coming in and ready to harvest every couple of weeks. There is a little more to succession planting than just staggering the plants though. It also includes planting different vegetables in succession, pairing vegetables in the same spot, and planting the same vegetables that have different maturity rates.

When determining which vegetables to plant in succession, start with crops that have a shorter growing season. Once the first crops have grown and are harvested, the second crops can be replanted in the same spot. During the time that you are planting, you can also seed other early-season vegetables. You can do this by intercropping, which is planting different crops in between row spaces. Selecting crops with different maturity dates can assist with staggered harvesting. Different maturity rates are available for early, mid, and late-season planting. The estimated time to maturity can usually be found on the seed packaging.

There are several things that you can do to help make your succession planting successful. Adding some compost to planting beds or in between them helps to keep your soil rich. Before you begin planting you will also need to make sure that you have enough seeds to get you all the way through the growing season. If you are planning to plant in hoop houses over winter, make sure that you have enough fresh or saved seeds to germinate.

If you have saved seeds in mid-spring you can start new transplants after your first batch has been planted. If you do not start by germinating seeds, the next best option for successful succession planting is to plant varieties of the same crop that will mature at different rates. You can also get a jump start on cooler weather crops by starting your seeds in the summer and keeping your soil cool.

Crop rotation

Whether or not you choose to stagger your planting, you should practice crop rotation. Rotating crops is the practice of growing different types of crops in subsequent seasons. Crop rotation helps to not deplete the soil of valuable nutrients and reduces soil erosion. It also helps to increase the fertility of the soil and produce more crop yield.

When farmers grow the same crops in the same plot of land year after year, a practice known as monocropping, it depletes the soil of nutrients and the crops cannot thrive. When crops are rotated it gives the soil a chance to recover the depleted nutrients. Crop rotation can also help deter certain pests and diseases from returning every year to the one plant that they are attracted to. Additionally, you can rotate crops in large fields or smaller plots, making it perfect for homesteading.

You must also consider how one crop will leave the condition of the soil before determining what to plant next. A crop that leaches one type of nutrient should always be followed by a crop that replenishes that nutrient. There is no hard and fast rule which limits the crops that you should use in a rotation. You can plan your crop rotation years and seasons in advance, or you can do it last minute once you have determined the condition of the soil.

Crop rotation can also include mixed farming or the incorporation of livestock. Livestock produces manure, which is packed full of essential nutrients that helps the soil to thrive. Residue produced from crops also provide food for the livestock, it comes full cycle.

Below I have included a basic guide to help you successfully rotate your crops, starting with the initial plant you are farming, followed by what you should follow it up with, and then lastly, what you should not follow it with.

Initial Plant	Follow up with	Do not follow with
Beans	Cauliflower, carrots, broccoli, cabbage, corn	Onions, garlic
Beets	Spinach	NA
Carrots	Lettuce, tomatoes	Dill
Cole crops (Brassica)	Beans, onions	Tomatoes
Cucumbers	Peas, radishes	Potatoes
Kale	Beans, peas	Brassicas
Lettuce	Carrots, cucumbers, radishes	NA
Onions	Radishes, lettuce, brassicas	Beans
Peas	Brassicas, carrots, beans, corn	NA
Potatoes	Beans, cabbage, corn, turnips	Tomatoes, squash, pumpkins
Radishes	Beans	Brassicas
Tomatoes	Carrots, onions	Brassicas

A simple crop rotation might look something like this:

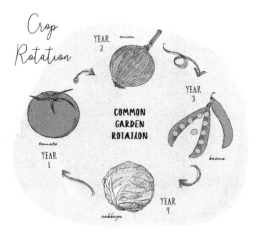

Chapter Summary

In order to have a successful homestead, you need to plan in advance. Having a plan for your property helps you utilize it to its full potential. When planning, you need to determine what kind of plants you are going to cultivate and where they will be placed. Planning out your crops makes your homestead more efficient and your property more effective. If you do not properly plan then this can lead to a waste of both time and resources.

Start by developing a planting plan before you purchase seeds. This can easily be done by drawing out a map of your property. During your initial planning phase you will need to determine the following: How much space you have to use for your crops (and anything else that you will be producing), what you and your family like to eat and want to grow, and the amount of food you will need to produce to feed your family.

You should also consider your planting schedule, any potential issues that could arise, and when you will be harvesting your crops. Finally, you should include in your plan how you intend to preserve the harvest that you produce.

Determining what you are going to plant is

dependent upon the location and growing zone of your property. Common categories of vegetables to grow include: leafy greens, legumes, nightshades, vine crops, root vegetables, and Brassicas. You might also consider growing a variety of fruits and incorporating various livestock.

Once you have developed a plan for utilizing your property to its fullest potential, the next step is to systematize your processes. If you plan on selling anything you produce, you should keep records of your processes. This way, in subsequent years, you will be able to produce the same type of results from your crops.

You can keep an effective planting schedule by utilizing plant phenology; incorporating both cold-season and warm-season vegetables; and also by using both staggered and succession planting methods and rotating your crops. Maintaining healthy soil is also important in enabling you to produce a bounty of food all year round. All of these practices can help you use your property to its fullest potential.

CHAPTER THREE
Preparing Your Ground and Planting

THE QUALITY OF your soil depends on where you live, what has been there before, and how you prepare it for planting. Before you dig or buy your first bag of soil, your planting activities need to be carefully thought out. Then you can get your soil ready for planting and set up your garden beds.

In this chapter, we are going to cover everything you could ever want to know about preparing your ground for planting. How the quality of your soil evolves over time is incredibly important to the health of your plants. You will learn how to remedy your soil with certain additives and how to build it up when you experience nutrient deficiencies. We will address soil aeration and various ways of planting, as well as different solutions that will allow for different planting methods. Some methods of planting are more ideal than others.

Also addressed in this chapter is the placement of your farming plots to ensure that your plants get adequate sunlight and water. Your watering system is very important and how you set it up can have a huge impact on the health of your crops. We will go over how you can maximize your space and crop yield with container gardening, raised beds, and planting directly into the ground, as well as everything you need to know about seeds, germination, and furrows.

Finally, we will cover composting, mulching, cover crops, crop rotation, and succession planting. By the end of this chapter, you should be fully equipped with everything you could possibly need to know about how to get the most out of your soil.

Types of Soil

Before we dive into all of the different aspects of creating a successful farm starting with your soil, let's take a quick look at the different types of soil. Soil is made up of both organic and inorganic materials which vary as a result of structure and composition. If you have never had a garden or farmed before, you probably haven't given much thought to the quality of the soil that you walk on. What you might not realize is that soil is actually a very complex structure. Soil is its own little ecosystem that provides a medium for the growth of vegetation and beneficial bacteria.

Soil is composed of many different materials, both organic and inorganic, and takes years to develop.

Inorganic materials are things that are not living such as rocks and minerals. Organic materials, however, were once alive and can include things like plants, animals, and bugs that have decomposed back into the soil.

The six main types of soil include sandy, clay, silt, peat, chalk, and loam. However, most soils are a combination of different materials, and as a homesteader, you will want a combination type of soil that is nutrient-dense and promotes growth.

Sandy soil, although low in nutrient content, is very easy to work with. Sandy soil also warms up quickly in the spring and has relatively quick water drainage. The nutrient content of this type of soil can easily be boosted with the addition of organic matter, such as compost. Clay soil, however, is much the opposite of sandy soil in that it has a high nutrient content but is very heavy and takes much longer to dry out. It stays cold and wet for much longer periods of time. Clay soil is also very slow to drain and is not ideal for many farmers and gardeners.

Silt soil is one of the most ideal soils to use for gardening. It is a light soil that is able to hold moisture and it drains well. One of the biggest disadvantages of silt is that it can easily be washed away by the rain; however, adding some organic matter can help with binding. Peat soil, on the other hand, is mostly made up of organic matter and retains moisture well. Peat soil is not naturally occurring and is often imported to provide an optimal base for planting gardens.

The last of the six main soil types are chalk soil and

loam soil. Chalk soil is highly alkaline and contains high amounts of lime or calcium carbonate. This type of soil is not conducive to growing plants that thrive in acidic soil. Farmers should only use chalk soil for plants that thrive in alkaline environments. Loam soil is a man-made mixture of sand, silt, and clay which was developed to combat the negative aspects of each of the soils. This type of soil is easy to work with, provides adequate drainage, and is fertile. Depending on the overall makeup of the soil, loam soil can be either sandy or more clay-like. Generally speaking, loam soil is the best type of soil for farming and gardening, however, plants can still benefit from being topped with additional organic matter.

Soil Quality

Now that you know the different types of soil that there are, it is time to determine what type of soil you have on your property. If you are not sure, you can take a sample of your soil using a soil testing kit and test your soil's pH quality for nitrogen, phosphorus, and potassium. Testing your soil before you start planting, and then periodically afterwards, can help you catch any deficiencies in the soil before they get too far. When you are aware of nutrient deficiencies in the soil, you can act quickly so that you are producing the healthiest plants possible. Soil testing can also provide you with information on the acidity or alkalinity of your soil, the percentage of organic matter that is present in your soil, and your soil's texture.

While it might take years of planting and harvesting for the nutrients in the soil to become depleted, you don't want to get to that point. Just as with your health, you want to take preventative measures to ensure that you are providing your soil and your plants with the best possible nutrients to survive and thrive. When plants are lacking nutrients they aren't going to scream for attention in the traditional sense, but they will begin to show you that something is wrong.

There are two different ways to keep your soil healthy. You can either work to evolve the soil quality over a period of time or you can do treatments in conjunction with planting and care maintenance. When I first moved onto my homestead, I didn't plant a single seed that entire first year. I did this because I knew upon testing the soil that it was of very poor quality. The previous owners did not know how to properly care for their soil and it took me an entire year of testing, composting, aerating, and fertilizing, in order to improve the quality of my soil enough to plant in it. My other option was to say "to heck with it," then start planting and continually work to improve the soil while I was growing things. This is entirely up to you, though, and greatly depends on the current health of your soil. If the health of your soil isn't too bad, then this is a great option. You might not get optimal growth in the first year, but you will still get a crop yield from your efforts. In the first year, I did opt for some container gardening so that I didn't have to buy all of my food (more on that in a minute).

Soil Remedy and Building

Once you have determined what your soil is lacking, you can easily come up with a plan to build up the health of your soil.

There are many things that you can add to your soil to improve the overall health. Building up your soil and adding natural and synthetic additives can make your whole growing process easier and more successful. Adding soil amendments is a little different than just adding a fertilizer. While fertilizers add nutrients to the soil, adding a soil amendment changes the condition of the soil, thus making it easier to work with. When the overall condition of the soil is changed, the roots of the plant are able to penetrate the soil easier and there is improved water filtration. An effective amendment of the soil also increases the availability of nutrients that are added to it.

When you are cultivating a new garden or farming plot, you should mix the soil amendments into the soil well before planting ever begins. If you are working with a piece of land that already has growth, then the amendments can be added directly on top of the soil and then watered so they soak in. However, you should not use amendments as a substitute for fertilizers but rather to increase the impact of fertilizers.

There are several different types of soil amendments: organic matter, lime, elemental sulfur, ammonium sulfate, and gypsum. Each one of them has a different role to play.

Modifying soil pH

To restore the pH balance of soil you can use lime. It is especially beneficial with acidic soils and is a great source of calcium. It works well on lawn grasses and other types of plants. Alternatively, if you have issues with your soil being too alkaline, you can add elemental sulfur. Elemental sulfur can slowly lower the soil's pH level and can be applied directly to the soil or mixed in with water. Ammonium sulfate, however, also works well to repair soil and it lowers the pH quicker than elemental sulfur, while also adding nitrogen and sulfur to the soil.

Nutrient deficiencies

Gypsum is different than the other amendments because it does not alter the pH of the soil. If the pH of the soil is fine even though other factors are off, the addition of gypsum can help. Gypsum improves water infiltration, promotes easier root penetration, and loosens soil that contains compacted clay. Additionally, Gypsum also helps to add calcium to the soil, improving its overall structure, and is great for plants with a higher need for calcium.

Organic matter, which includes materials that have been fully composted, helps to improve the soil's ability to hold onto water and nutrients, while also increasing beneficial microorganisms. Adding in some earthworm castings (also known as worm poop) is a great way to amend your soil.

Fertilizers

If you have incorporated livestock into your homestead, then you should have plenty of access to fresh high-quality organic fertilizer. Organic in this case simply means that the nutrients in the fertilizer come from the by-products, or remains, of an organism. One of the most readily available organic fertilizers on a homestead is animal manure. However, this can also mean the by-product of the solids from your composting toilet, cottonseed meal, earthworm castings, blood meal, fish emulsion, sewage sludge, and other forms of compost.

One of the biggest downfalls about using fresh organic fertilizers that do not come pre-packaged is that they aren't labeled with the exact nutrient ratios. Organic fertilizers thrive off of being in soil that is warm and moist, which allows the microorganisms to be active and break down in order to release nutrients into the soil.

With organic fertilizers, the nutrient release takes place over longer periods of time rather than happening quickly. One of the downfalls to this is that the plant might not get the nutrients it needs, when it needs them. Unlike other organic fertilizers, manure is a complete fertilizer; however, the overall nutrient supply is low. Fresh manure is always best as it has the highest nutrient content. If the manure is composted, weathered, or aged, the nutrient content decreases. Typical sources of manure include horses, cows, pigs, chickens, and sheep.

While organic fertilizers are generally low in nutrients, they do offer a lot of other benefits to soil health. Organic fertilizers increase the overall organic matter in the soil, and as I mentioned earlier, this can change the actual composition of the soil. Increased organic matter in the soil improves both the water-holding ability of the soil and the soil's physical structure, allowing the roots of the plant to get more air. Organic fertilizers also do not pollute water supplies like synthetic fertilizers do and are slow to leach nutrients from the soil.

Another type of fertilization method is called foliar feeding. This is where a liquid fertilizer is sprayed directly onto the plant and the essential elements are absorbed through its leaves, much like when you rub topical ointment onto your skin. The absorption takes place through the skin of the leaves and the stomata, or the plant's pores. Even plants with bark can absorb nutrients via foliar feeding.

Soil Aeration

Aerating your soil allows air, water, and other nutrients to penetrate deeper into the soil. This, in turn, helps to produce a stronger more vibrant plant. If you have soil that is compact, there are several ways in which you can aerate it for better nutrient absorption.

A very easy way to aerate your soil is to use a broad fork, which has several vertical spikes that are attached to a horizontal plate. The spikes are stuck into the ground in order to poke holes into the soil to let in more air. A broad fork is better to use than a rototiller as it does not disturb the ecology of the soil and it helps microorganisms remain undisturbed. With the use of a broad fork, you can plant seeds and seedlings and aerate the soil after planting without essentially replanting everything. Broad forks can also be used to harvest root vegetables quickly and easily without damaging the soil.

Plot Placement

The plot placement of your crops is going to greatly depend on how much land you have, what you are going to plant, and if you are also going to include livestock on your homestead. With your plots properly thought out, even on a half-acre of land, you can produce up to 50 pounds of wheat, 280 pounds of pork, 120 dozen eggs, 100 pounds of honey, 25 to 75 pounds of nuts, 600 pounds of fruit, and over 2,000 pounds of vegetables in just one year. That is a lot of food!

While many traditional farmers plant in rows, there is an easy way to get three times the amount of produce in the same square foot space. Four feet of garden space plotted in a staggered, wide-bed planting scheme still takes up the same amount of space as a 4-foot-long row, but with three times the yield.

Watering/Irrigation System

While you can certainly walk around with a large watering can to water your crops, there are much better ways that will save you a lot of time (and your back for that matter). Water is how nutrients from the soil are drawn up through the plants' roots and stems and fed into the leaves, fruits, and vegetables. Planning your irrigation methods is essential to your garden's survival. The traditional methods of watering from the top down are not very effective.

When plants are watered using the traditional top-down method, the water normally only penetrates about an inch into the soil. This prevents the water from being fully absorbed by the roots of the plant. Watering the plants directly and keeping their leaves moist also makes them more susceptible to pests and diseases. If you are going to water plants from the top down always make sure to water the base of the plant and not the actual leaves. You can help reduce evaporation when watering from the top down by placing a layer of mulch on top of the soil.

You can also automate your watering process by using drip irrigation. Drip irrigation will deliver water directly where it is needed to the plant and can either be consistent or it can be set on a timer. All drip irrigation systems should include these three things: a timer to ensure your crops are being watered at the appropriate times, a water filter to prevent particles from clogging up the system, and a pressure regulator to ensure that the water pressure does not become too much for the system to handle, which is about 10-30 psi for smaller gardens and can be adjusted according to size.

The actual tubing used for the irrigation system is generally a half-inch of polyurethane supply tubing. The tubing can either be laid on top of the soil or buried within the garden itself. This is the part you run along the garden which feeds water to some smaller tubing that does the actual watering of the plants.

You can construct a very simple homemade soaker hose irrigation system by installing a hose with holes punched in it right on top of the soil. Then just turn it on at certain times of the day. You can also take a plastic bottle, poke holes in the sides and bury the bottle next to your plants, leaving the cap exposed. Simply add water to the bottle periodically as the water seeps out into the plants' roots.

Whenever you are watering by hand or using a method where you bury bottles for irrigation purposes, try to use collected rainwater. This is a great way to save on your water and add additional nutrients to your plants.

Container Gardening

Container gardening is a great option if you lack space (which you shouldn't on a homestead) or want to add a new way of gardening to your homestead. Containers are great for growing ornamental plants, herbs, and flowers. There are several advantages to using container gardening. For example, you don't have to worry about having good quality soil on the property since you can purchase your own, the plots are small and easy to manage, plants in containers are less susceptible to pests and disease, and you really don't have to worry about weeds.

One of the biggest disadvantages of container gardens is that they need to be watered frequently. Excessive watering can strip the soil of essential nutrients so the plants in containers need to be fertilized often.

You can easily solve the problem of having to water the plants too often by creating a self-watering system. This can be done by creating a reservoir in the bottom of the pot with a wicking system so the plants can get water on demand. This also helps with nutrients being leached from the soil.

Another benefit of container gardening is that there is not as much soil as there is with in-ground planting so the soil can heat up faster. This gives the plants that love warmer soil the ability to quickly get growing. There is also the advantage of moving the plants indoors if it gets too cold, giving you the ability to grow produce year-round.

While you might hear that you won't get the best vegetables if you grow them in a container, this is simply not true. You can grow amazing vegetables, herbs, and flowers in containers which can turn out even better than if grown in the ground. Here is a list of vegetables and other produce that you can successfully grow in containers:

- ☒ Tomatoes
- ☒ Beans
- ☒ Lettuce and salad greens
- ☒ Peppers and Chillies
- ☒ Radishes
- ☒ Asian Greens
- ☒ Spinach
- ☒ Peas
- ☒ Carrots
- ☒ Cucumber
- ☒ Squash
- ☒ Potatoes
- ☒ Squash
- ☒ Herbs
- ☒ Medicinal plants
- ☒ Eggplant

While the success of your container garden will greatly depend on you caring for it, you should also make sure that you are giving the plants enough room to grow. Any type of vining plant should have a trundle or vertical structure in the pot that will allow it to climb up.

Raised Beds

There are many advantages of planting your seeds in a wide, deep, raised bed other than offering a good growing environment. Due to the higher ratio of garden bed space to space for you to walk, you are able to grow more vegetables with less room which then maximizes your garden area.

One advantage to raised beds that many gardeners enjoy is that after the first year they tend to be less work. Raised beds are easier to weed, fertilize, and water. Whereas a traditional garden needs to have walking space between each row, it is not necessary for a raised bed garden. Paths in a raised bed garden are only used for walking, while in a traditional garden you might have to worry about getting some type of large machinery in there for cultivation.

There are two different types of raised beds: those that are directly in the ground and those that are supported by boards. Raised beds that are directly in the ground are simply mounds of loose soil that have been well-prepared and are usually six to eight inches high. Beds that are directly in the ground are re-formed every time you plant, whereas permanent raised beds are built with stones, blocks, or wood.

Either type of raised bed can be beneficial to the growing process if you are working with soil that is heavy or does not drain very well. Permanent raised beds are almost like planting inside of large containers. Permanent raised beds are great for home gardeners and are easy to work with using hand tools. With raised beds, the soil never really compacts like traditional in-ground planting since no one is stepping onto the beds. This allows the soil to remain porous and loose. Having consistent loose soil allows for good water drainage, and also allows air, fertilizer, and water to easily get to the plant roots.

Additionally, with permanent raised beds, the walking paths between the beds are also low maintenance. Considering that they are mainly used for walking and nothing gets planted there, the paths stay dry, clean, and free of weeds. Permanent raised beds also make crop rotation extremely easy. Simple crop rotation prevents nutrients from getting leached out of the soil and keeps pests at bay. Raised bed gardens are also very beautiful and they are easy to maintain and keep organized.

You can easily create raised beds in the ground by using string or stakes to mark off where you want them to go. Raised beds can vary in size from 16 inches to 4 feet wide, with walkways about 20 inches wide. Simply pull up the soil from the sides of the bed into the middle, mixing in all of the organic materials with a sturdy metal rake. Use the back of the rake to level off the bed while ensuring the sides slope at about a 45-degree angle.

Planting Directly Into the Ground

While many homesteaders prefer to use seedlings for planting, some still prefer to plant directly into the ground. In order to be successful with planting seeds directly into the ground, you need to ensure that the soil is properly prepared. Adding manure, compost, or both to the soil will help to keep it rich and ripe for planting. You can add manure and compost to the soil by rototilling it in or by using another way to turn the soil.

Once your soil is adequately prepared, it is time to actually sow the seeds. One of the easiest ways to sow seeds is to draw a line or make a little trench in the soil with your finger and simply drop the seeds into the trench. This should be simple if your soil is properly prepared. Don't worry about adding too many seeds as you will likely thin them out afterwards. When you are finished putting your seeds into the soil, cover them and gently pat the soil down to ensure that the seeds are in good contact with the surrounding soil.

Once your seeds have been sown, give them a good watering. This is when top watering works well. Make sure that you are using a watering can that will disburse the water evenly rather than put out a stream that will disturb the seeds. Don't forget to mark the trench where you planted your seeds, you won't want to forget what you planted there!

Seeds vs. Seedlings

There are two ways in which you can plant your produce, either by sowing seeds directly into your container, raised bed, or the ground, or by planting seedlings (which are also known as plugs) that have already started to grow. Purchasing seeds is more cost-effective than purchasing seedlings or plants. However, working with plants or seedlings can save you a bit of time since the growing process is already underway.

Many farmers opt to create their own seedlings or plugs but sowing seeds in plug trays. Trays typically come with 200 plug holes where you put one seed into each hole or plug cell. The shape of the cell encourages the seeds to grow roots that bind well to the soil.

You can start your seedlings in just about any kind of shallow container. Bonus points if you can transplant a biodegradable container directly into the ground. You can also start seedlings in specially made pots that offer additional nutrients which will make transplanting your plants easier.

Peat pots are good for larger seeds and plants that don't normally like to be transplanted. Peat pots are good for germinating, growing, and transplanting plants. Peat pellets are similar to peat pots but need to be placed in water to be activated. Whether you are using a container from your kitchen to start your plants or purchasing a special type of planting medium, you need to ensure that the containers have good drainage. Some of the ideal growing mediums to use when starting seeds are peat moss, sphagnum moss, vermiculite, perlite, and of course soil directly from your garden.

Preparing Seeds to Germinate

There are techniques that you can use to help your seeds germinate more quickly and more effectively. Three of these techniques are known as scarification, soaking, and stratification.

Scarification simply means to make a mark on the outside of the seed with a knife or file, allowing the seed to germinate faster. To soak the seeds, place them in hot water overnight and then sow them the next day after the water has cooled. Stratification is what you might remember from germinating seeds in grade school. You can use either peat moss, vermiculite, or even a damp paper towel. Place the seeds inside a plastic bag with your growing medium and place it in a warm place. Soon you will see the initial roots start to grow and sprout.

Indoor germination

In order to germinate seeds indoors, you need three things: light, warmth, and moisture. Light can come from either natural sources, such as a sunny windowsill, or from the use of artificial light sources such as cool-white fluorescent bulbs. Make sure to turn the seedlings periodically so that they get sun and have light exposure evenly on all sides.

Warmth is also important for proper seed germination. Seedlings thrive in a temperature that remains 70 to 75 degrees Fahrenheit. Proper moisture and humidity ratios are also vital for effective germination. Whatever medium you are using to germinate your seeds, make sure to keep it moist but never soaking wet. You can help to create the perfect germination environment by covering the seed tray with a piece of glass to create a warming environment. Once the seeds begin to germinate, you can then remove the glass.

As the seeds begin to germinate, check the seedlings every couple of days to ensure that the growing medium is not drying out. If it is lighter in color, water the seedlings from the ground up. This helps to avoid disrupting the seedlings when watering from the top. Once the first real leaves of the seedlings begin to develop, start fertilizing the plants. Once the seedlings are mature enough, you can begin top watering.

Germinating your plants indoors also means that you will need to transplant them into the ground, a container, or a raised bed. If you have started the seedlings in flats you will need to transplant them to larger containers before putting them into their final planting plot. Before transplanting the seedlings into their final planting plot, expose them to the outdoor elements. This can be done by placing them on a porch or deck on cloudy and sunny days. A place with a nice breeze will also help to strengthen their stems.

Tilling and Cultivating

Tilling your soil helps to prepare and cultivate the land for planting. Tilling the soil simply means to break up and loosen the soil to prepare it for planting. Cultivating the soil also includes removing weeds from the soil. Tilling and loosening the soil allows for aeration and allows nutrients, water, and air to penetrate the soil deeper, promoting growth.

Cultivating and tilling the soil breaks up the top layer that might be dried out and crusty, which helps get all of the good stuff to the root of the plant. While everyone knows that plants need to be watered, it is also essential for air to get to the roots as well. This helps the micro-organisms in the soil thrive so that they can do all of their essential tasks such as helping to improve the soil quality and creating more nutrients for the plants.

When the soil is properly tilled and cultivated, it allows the seeds to germinate more successfully since it is less difficult for them to break through the top layer of soil.

Tilling the soil also helps to bring weeds up to the surface, making it easier to get rid of them. This also helps to interrupt the germination of the weed seeds within the soil. When weeds are eliminated, the water and nutrients are preserved for the plants that you actually planted rather than the weeds stealing all of the good stuff. Not to mention that it is just more aesthetically pleasing to have a plot that is not covered in weeds.

Tilling is a form of soil cultivation that is necessary when either preparing a new garden bed or when adding large amounts of organic material. When cultivating, the soil must be loosened for the first couple of inches and tilling helps to get deeper down into the soil. However, you don't want to go too deep as this will cause the top layer of soil to dry out faster. If you are cultivating around things that you have already planted, you must be careful not to disturb the roots of the plants as this will damage them. If you have already planted and are cultivating the soil, make sure to go between the rows without getting too close to the plants themselves.

You can shallow cultivate your plots when the soil is looking dry and cracked and the weeds are coming up to the surface. You should not cultivate your soil when it is wet. Cultivating and tilling soil that is too wet will only cause the soil to become compact making it more difficult for water, air, and nutrients to reach the roots of the plant. You should also cultivate your soil before you start to plant directly into the ground. This is particularly helpful when you are working with smaller seeds as they have a more difficult time sprouting if the soil is too dry or compacted.

You can also shallow cultivate the soil by adding things like compost or organic fertilizer to it. This helps to loosen up the top layer of soil and get the nutrients mixed in while helping to reduce rain runoff. This also helps to jumpstart the process of worms and other microorganisms so they can do their thing and provide more nutrients to the soil.

While shallow cultivation only affects the first inch or so of the soil, tilling will cultivate the soil about 8-10 inches deep. If you are working with soil that is of very poor quality, then you can cultivate even deeper. If you are mixing soil amendments into your beds, then you can till the first 4-8 inches; but it is best to do this at the end of the growing season. Tilling over the fall and winter months allows the amendments more time to fully decompose rather than being mixed in with plants and seeds right away. This greatly benefits the soil for the next growing season. Then when spring arrives, you can till the beds as you normally would to prepare them for planting.

Tilling is a very important aspect of farming since the soil will become compacted over the years due to foot traffic, rain, and other factors. When you loosen the soil, you allow air to penetrate deeper into the soil which also benefits the microorganisms. Tilling the soil and loosening it up also provides a better environment for plant roots to spread out, making it easier for plants to get nutrients out of the soil and water. This is especially important if you have clay in your soil and it is difficult for plants to get adequate air.

Digging Furrows

A furrow is a trench created in the soil or garden bed, made with a plow or other type of agricultural instrument. It allows for planting crops and helps with irrigation and walking pathways within planted beds. Once a furrow is dug, seeds and fertilizer are added and then the furrow is closed up. Digging furrows are beneficial when you are dealing with topsoil layers that are a bit dryer as furrows allow the seeds to get deeper into the more moist soil.

When you dig a furrow in your soil you are helping to slow the water runoff and improve the soil permeability where the top layer, or fertile soil, may have been eroded or blown away by the wind. Furrows are great when you want to side dress a crop, or add fertilizer right next to it rather than directly on top of the soil. You can do this by digging a furrow, adding fertilizer, and then burying the fertilizer. You might also dig a furrow to move water irrigation systems around. You can utilize a furrow no matter what size plots you are planting.

Using furrow irrigation also provides greater

flexibility when utilizing crop rotation practices. It allows for more effective water management and lends to soil improvement. While digging furrows can be a larger time investment, you don't need to worry about investing too much financially other than purchasing a garden hoe. This method can be used for just about any soil type, making it a very widely used method for soil cultivation.

What to put in a furrow and overtop the soil

There are certain crops that benefit from furrows more than others. These include plants that are prone to higher levels of damage when their stems or crowns become covered with water, such as tomatoes, root vegetables, potatoes, and beans. Furrows are also beneficial when growing vine crops like grapes and fruit trees. In the early planting stages, the furrow can be dug alongside the trees or vines to improve and hold water spread. Other crops that benefit from the use of furrows include:

- ☒ Corn
- ☒ Sunflowers
- ☒ Sugarcane
- ☒ Rice
- ☒ Wheat
- ☒ Soybeans

Crops that are grown using the furrow irrigation method tolerate excessive watering better than those grown in flat soil. This is because when the water is drained it helps to re-aerate the soil. Lands that are uniformly flat or slightly sloped are the best for using furrows which can help prevent soil erosion from excess rainfall or irrigation.

In order to prevent erosion, you can also add mulch to the topsoil of the furrows. This allows water to filter through the mulch and soak into the soil below.

Row planting

With digging furrows, you will also be row planting. This simply means that you are planting your seeds in a straight line. This is the most traditional way of growing vegetables. The spacing between the rows should remain uniform while the space between the plants within the rows will be determined by the size of the plant.

Planting in rows can help keep your crops clean and organized and visually appealing. Larger vining plants tend to grow better when planted in rows since it allows their vines room to freely grow. Row planting is also beneficial if you are using any kind of machinery to plant or harvest your crops.

One of the biggest disadvantages of row planting is that it can take up a lot of space which will ultimately decrease your harvest. It also requires accurate spacing which can take a lot of time to do. And unless you are using an irrigation system, watering can become a little complicated.

Broadcast seeding

Broadcast seeding is the opposite of row planting as it involves scattering the seeds, by hand or mechanically, over a large area. The seeds can then be lightly buried within the soil by raking over them. Crops planted in this manner will require up to 20% more seeds than crops planted using other methods, which is why it is used more for planting cover crops and grass seed.

Spreading compost, manure, fertilizer, and vermiculite

Adding compost, manure, fertilizer, and vermiculite to your soil will help to improve the soil's structure and add beneficial nutrients. Adding these components will increase nutrient and water retention and aerate the soil, which results in a more robust and healthier plant. You can easily add compost, manure, fertilizer, and or vermiculite to soil by throwing it in the furrow with the seeds and then raking the remaining soil over the top. If you are looking to keep the top of the soil moist, you can also add more directly on top of the furrows after you have planted.

Mulching

Mulch can include straw, grass clippings, wood chips, chopped leaves, and even compost. The purpose of mulch is for the organic material to break down and add nutrients to the soil. Adding mulch also helps keep the soil moist, prevents weeds, and protects the plant's roots. It does not, however, protect from pests and diseases.

Depending on the time of year, you will need varying amounts of mulch; less in the summer and more during the cold months. It is best to apply organic mulch in the early summer months or the beginning of spring. You can re-mulch and apply a thicker layer come late fall. Having a good amount of mulch covering the ground around your plants can also help to ease drastic freezing and thawing cycles.

Before you start mulching, you first need to remove any existing weeds. You don't want them to start growing under the mulch. If at all possible, remove any existing mulch before laying down new stuff. If you are unable to remove the old mulch, you can use the same or similar kind.

Once you have added the mulch, rake over the area to even it out. Finally, water it enough so that the water is able to soak through into the ground below. It is best to replace organic mulch every year as it is meant to break down. There are also fewer nutrients present in mulch that has been there for a while.

Composting

When using compost, you need to ensure that it is cured and finished before adding it to your crops. If you add compost too soon it might stress the plants and stall their growth. If you are using compost as mulch instead of directly mixing it in with your soil, then you don't have to worry about the compost being finished.

Curing compost, which means to condition it, is used with hot composting. The compost essentially goes through fermentation using a process called aerobic decomposition in which bacteria that thrives on air breaks down organisms. The process of composting organic matter creates the ideal environment for micro-organisms to multiply.

The compost is cured and ready to use when the inside temperature of the compost is the same as the temperature in the surrounding environment. Curing the compost allows for beneficial microorganisms and fungi to progress within the compost, breaking down organic matter.

The amount of space you use for your compost depends on how much you are ultimately making. Generally, the more compost the better. While you can certainly use a tumbling composter, the simplest and most economical way to produce compost is just to pick a spot on the ground and start there. You can build a caged-in area of four posts and some chicken wire to keep the compost all in one spot while still allowing for good airflow.

Cover crops

Cover crops are used to help manage the erosion of soil, increase soil fertility and quality, manage weeds, pests, and diseases, and increase the biodiversity of the ecosystem. Cover crops can grow over the winter and be used as an off-season crop after the main crops have been harvested.

Companion planting

Companion planting involves the pairing of different plants that work well together. An example of this would be planting corn, pole beans, and squash together. The corn provides support for the beans to climb, the leaves of the squash hug the soil and decrease water evaporation and weeds, and the pole beans provide nitrogen to the soil. Some of the other benefits of companion planting include:

- Healthier plants through the use of symbiotic relationships.
- An increase in overall production yield.
- The ability to decrease insect predators and diseases.
- The attraction of beneficial organisms and insects.

Green manure

Green manure crops are similar to cover crops. While cover crops are meant to be harvested, green manure crops are grown specifically to be dug back into the soil for the continued improvement of its fertility. Green manure benefits the soil by drawing the nutrients out of it and storing it in the cells and roots of the plant. When the green manure is harvested it is dug back into the soil where the nutrients are slowly released. These nutrients then become available to the next crop that is planted in that plot.

Chapter Summary

The quality of your soil can dramatically impact the success of your crops. Even if you do not have great soil already on your land, there are many things that you can do to improve the structure of the soil and grow a successful harvest.

Before doing anything to your soil you need to determine what type of soil you are working with. In order to improve the health of your soil you may need to add certain amendments to it. Modify the pH of soil by adding things like organic matter, lime, elemental sulfur, ammonium sulfate, and or gypsum. Many of these also have the added benefits of replacing deficient nutrients in the soil.

In order for soil to remain healthy, it needs adequate irrigation, aeration, and additional nutrients.

You can plant your seeds in various ways, such as in containers, raised beds, or directly into the ground using furrows. You can also speed up with the growing process by germinating your seeds in advance. This can easily be done indoors by placing your seedlings on a sunny windowsill or by using artificial lighting.

Tilling and cultivating your soil helps to provide adequate aeration and prepare the soil for adding large amounts of organic matter. Planting your crops in rows is one of the most common practices. You can also add mulch to help keep your soil moist, prevent weeds, and protect your plants' roots.

The next chapter will focus on the care and harvesting of your bounty.

CHAPTER FOUR
Care and Harvesting Your Bounty

N OW THAT YOUR plots are ready to be planted, it is time to learn all about caring for and maintaining your crops, and what to do when it comes time to harvest. This chapter will cover what to do on a day-to-day basis, such as gardening practices, and will include specialty situations, trouble-shooting, and making adjustments as conditions change. It will also cover harvesting.

You will learn what you need to look for when walking your garden, and the things that you should do if you run into any issues. This chapter will also cover how to determine the best time of day to water your plants, how to monitor their response, and any additional feeding of your plants that you will need to do, including what to feed them, how much, and how often.

Additionally, you will learn how to prune and thin

certain plants, how to best support vining crops, and how to prevent or remedy weed situations. We will also take a look at common pests and what to do if you experience pest problems with your crops. Then, of course, there is the fun part of actually harvesting your crops.

Walking Your Garden

You should make it a point to walk your garden on a daily basis. Not only is it a good way to get exercise, it also gives you a snapshot of the health of your crops so that you can catch any unfavorable situations before they get out of hand. When you are walking your garden you should look for any discoloration of leaves, parts of the plant that look like there may be pests present, or any weeds that are popping up.

You can easily get rid of weeds by pulling them out as you go along your walk. However, don't throw them out as you can use them as part of your compost or even to feed your livestock. If you see any discoloration on your plants, you must first determine what is causing it, such as a lack of certain nutrients, and then seek to rectify the issue. If you are experiencing pest problems you must first determine which type of pest you are dealing with before coming up with a solution. It is best not to ignore any of these signs as acting sooner rather than later will only benefit your crops.

Watering Your Crops

There are a few tips and tricks when it comes to watering your crops that will help them to thrive. Although it is best to water them directly at the root with an irrigation hose, any watering is better than no watering at all.

Water your crops early in the morning, the ground is cooler and it will take longer for the soil to dry out.

Concentrate your watering at the base of the plants rather than directly on top of the plant and avoid getting the leaves wet.

- ☒ Avoid watering in the evening; this tends to draw more pests, disease, and fungus.
- ☒ Water your plants deeply rather than lightly to make sure enough of the soil gets wet.
- ☒ Watering more heavily less often is better than watering lightly more often.
- ☒ If possible, use an irrigation system with fixtures that are closer to the ground.
- ☒ Avoid using overhead sprinkler systems as most of the water never reaches the ground.
- ☒ Directly water trees every 7 to 10 days, directly at their base.
- ☒ You can use soaker hoses to get water directly to the base of the plant.
- ☒ Plants in containers should be watered about once per day, especially during dry weather.
- ☒ Plants in pots and other containers hold more heat and tend to dry out quicker.

☒ For raised beds and containers, lay down several inches of mulch and compost to keep soil cool and moist while also deterring weeds.

☒ Avoid watering soil directly as this can cause run-off.

Feeding Your Plants

Fertilizing your plants with various byproducts of your homestead can help to produce healthy and hearty crops. You can use fertilizers from your livestock or mix together a few things to create your own. Using high-quality and organic fertilizers are best. Organic in this form means fertilizer that is produced as a byproduct of your homestead which can include manure, fish emulsion, blood meal and anything else that is a byproduct of your livestock.

Fertilizers can be made from compost and other organic matter. You can even make liquid fertilizer that can be mixed with water for watering your crops. Here are just a few things that you can use to create high-quality fertilizer to feed to your plants:

☒ Blood or left over meat processing byproducts
☒ Compost
☒ Cottonseed meal
☒ Seaweed
☒ Soybeans
☒ Wood ash
☒ Worm castings

- ☒ Any kind of livestock manure
- ☒ Bone meal
- ☒ Blood meal
- ☒ Fish emulsion
- ☒ Fish meal
- ☒ Grass clippings
- ☒ Dried leaves

All of these things can add beneficial nutrients to your crops.

You can also make a compost tea very easily, which makes a great liquid fertilizer. You can make compost and strain it into a container and use the resulting liquid as compost tea.

You will want to be careful when figuring out how much fertilizer to give your crops; too much is worse than too little. You can give plants liquid fertilizer pretty much any time you are watering them. This form of fertilizer is milder and you won't have to worry about burning your plants if you use too much.

Here is a guide to help you determine how much or how little fertilizer to add to your soil:

Heavy Feeding Crops	Moderate Feeding Crops	Light Feeding Crops
Broccoli	Beets	Arugula
Brussel sprouts	Carrots	Bush beans
Cabbage	Okra	Mustard greens
Cauliflower	Pole beans	Peas
Corn	Potatoes	Southern peas
Cucumbers	Sweet potatoes	Turnips
Eggplant	Artichoke	Chicory
Kale	Garlic	Endive
Kohlrabi	Lettuce	Collard greens
Onions	Pumpkin	Herbs
Peppers	Radish	Parsnip
Rhubarb	Rutabaga	Swiss chard
Squash	Scallions	
Tomatoes	Zucchini	
Watermelon		

Pruning and Thinning Plants

Pruning and trimming your crops is important for several reasons. Pruning is best done in the dead of winter or early spring, never in the fall. There are not a lot of crops that actually need pruning, other than fruit trees. You should also make sure it is not damp outside when you are pruning your plants as this can actually increase the spread of disease.

Pruning is also great for allowing more sunlight through shrubs and trees. Pruning can be done when there is a dead branch or when branches are rubbing or crossing over each other. You can also prune branches that are very low and might interfere with foot traffic. It is better to prune as close to the base of the branch or stem as possible rather than further up.

Also, make sure that you are keeping your pruning tools clean as you don't want to cross-contaminate diseases between trees and branches. When thinning your plants it is better to take off the parts that are looking a little lax in the health department such as bruised, browning, or dead leaves, and produce that is not looking good.

Staking to Support Vining Plants and Other Crops

As mentioned in the previous chapter, planting certain crops in close proximity to each other can be mutually beneficial for each plant. Here are a few tips to remember regarding supportive companion planting combinations:

- ☒ Corn helps to provide support for the pole beans.
- ☒ Leaves of the squash hug the soil and decrease water evaporation and weeds.

- ☒ Pole beans provide nitrogen to the soil.
- ☒ Tomatoes work well with Brassicas.
- ☒ Avoid planting nightshades together.
- ☒ Low groundcover plants help to block weeds.

Using support structures

You can also maximize growing space by using a support structure, such as a trellis, with your vining plants. Support structures like trellises, bean teepees, and support stakes, help to increase growing space by allowing these plants to vine vertically. Just make sure that whatever you are using for a support structure is sturdy enough to support your plants and won't topple over. You can easily buy or build your own support structures.

There are several different kinds of trellises available to help support your crops:

- ☒ Arches
- ☒ Teepees or tripods
- ☒ Grids
- ☒ Fans
- ☒ A-frames or ladders

An arch trellis is shaped like a simple arch with some kind of pattern in the center to help support the vines. Arches are both decorative and functional and great for vining crops that don't get too heavy. Teepees and tripods are just as their names imply and are a very easy option to DIY. They are often seen being used for tomato plants. Grid trellises can easily attach to a wall or other structure to provide support for vining plants. This is a wonderful option if you are looking for functionality, privacy, or to help divide up a space.

A fan trellis is in a fan shape. It often has several long, vertical pieces. Finally, an A-frame is like a grid and ladder combined and is great for supporting heavier plants. You can easily build these with varying heights and lengths.

Preventing and Managing Weeds

Preventing and managing weeds on your homestead can help to ensure that your crops are thriving. Having weeds in your garden can steal precious nutrients from your crops, not to mention being an eyesore. There are several ways to prevent and remedy weeds taking over your crops.

One way to control weeds and also retain the moisture in your soil is by using mulch. Simply cover the soil where you have seeds planted with a thick layer of organic mulch. When you water, if you are watering top down, mulch helps to prevent soil erosion or runoff, while also deterring weeds from growing. Some of the best kinds of mulch to use to prevent weeds include straw, pine needles, and shredded black and white newspaper.

Earlier, I mentioned walking your garden on a daily basis. One of the advantages of doing this is to be able to pull weeds out as you see them. You will want to make the weeding of your crops very easy, which you can do by using raised beds.

You will also want to make sure that you are regularly attending to your garden, as you do not want weeds to prevent you from producing higher crop yields. Effectively weeding your crops can yield as much as six times healthier produce. It is best to weed your garden when the soil is drier or after a very heavy rain. Crops are generally more susceptible to competition from weeds in the early stages and right before plants begin to fruit.

Pest and Disease Prevention

Pests and diseases can ruin a crop. When you start walking your garden you should know what to look for to ensure that you catch any pests or diseases promptly. This is also another advantage of having crops in raised beds, as it discourages insects and pathogens from remaining in the soil over the winter months. This then deters them from infecting the crop for the next season.

There are many different kinds of pests and diseases that can strike plants. What to look for can help you determine how to best facilitate healing in your plants. Some of the key signs of pests and diseases in crops include:

- ☒ Holes directly through leaves.
- ☒ Scabby spots on fruits and leaves.
- ☒ Yellowing or discolored leaves.

☒ Coverings that look like mold or mildew on leaves or fruit.

If you find any of these in your crops you will need to determine exactly what the pest or disease is in order to rectify the situation. You can easily search online for a visual representation of what certain pests and diseases look like.

Some diseases and pests can be further prevented by not saving seeds, choosing resistant plant varieties, as well as not composting the leaves or other parts of the plant that may be infected.

How to Monitor Weather Conditions

While you might not have much control over weather conditions, it is important that you monitor the weather in order to optimize your crop yields. Weather is one of the single most important things that can affect crop growth, total yield, fertilization needs, and the occurrences of pests.

Being aware of the weather includes more than just figuring out if it is going to rain or not. Real-time weather conditions include not only rain, but also humidity, air, and dew temperature. When there are sudden and extreme changes in weather, such as frost, drought, hail, and flooding, this causes instant stress on the plants which can lead to failed production as well as wasted money.

The only way to completely prevent weather from

being a major determining factor is to grow your crops within a greenhouse or some other kind of indoor facility. However, if you are like most homesteaders, most of your crops will be grown outdoors without the added advantage of coverings. Therefore, your crop growth and its health is a direct reflection of the weather in your area.

There are many things that you can predict when factoring in the weather. For example, the combination of certain temperatures coupled with humidity can predict if you will have issues with certain pests or any occurrences of plant diseases. Based on the weather information that homesteaders receive, they can plan accordingly for sowing their seeds, protecting their crops, harvesting their yield, as well as other field activities, in an attempt to avoid any negative side effects from the weather.

When homesteaders are knowledgeable about their weather conditions they can use this information to help determine irrigation schedules and also know the best time to fertilize or protect their crops.

Mulching

I have mentioned in previous chapters the benefits of mulching. Mulching helps to insulate the soil and protects it from drastic weather changes. It can also keep the soil cooler during the hot summer months and warmer during the cold winter months.

Additionally, mulching helps to retain water and

keeps the soil and roots of the plant moist. Adding mulch on top of your soil also helps to keep weeds at bay without sucking vital nutrients from the soil. Mulching can even help to prevent against soil being too compacted by rainwater. When there is mulch over the soil, rainwater has to first pass through the mulch before being absorbed by the soil.

You can lay mulch directly on top of the soil around crops or within raised beds. If you are mulching around a tree, make sure not to put more mulch directly against the trunk of the tree. So often, I see trees that have piles of mulch directly at the base at an incline towards the trunk. You absolutely want to avoid this as it prevents the tree from being able to get adequate water to its roots. If you are going to mulch around a tree, make sure the mulch is further back and creates an open circle around the base of the tree.

How to extend the growing season

You can extend your growing season through the use of protected cultivation methods. These can help you by spreading out your workload over the seasons resulting in less stress during the hot summer months and more enjoyable farming during cooler weather. Of course, the ultimate goal is to increase overall crop yield. When you implement protected cultivation methods, frost dates become less important to you and you should technically be able to farm all year round.

Here are some things that you will need to extend your growing season:

Plant protectors: These can be anything from styrofoam coverings to tents that you place over raised beds. For smaller plants or those that are just budding, you can DIY your own plant protectors with things like milk jugs or two-liter bottles.

Hotbeds: These are very much like small greenhouses specifically used to keep a mass of compost warm and are used for starting plants rather than protecting them throughout the cold winter. Hotbeds and cold frames are generally constructed the same but used for different purposes.

Cold frames: These are generally small boxes that are placed over an area with a glass top. You can purchase these or easily make them from old windows. The purpose of a cold frame is to protect plants from weather conditions.

Hot caps: A hot cap is very similar to a plant protector while the main difference here is that hot caps allow sunlight through as a source of heat for the plant.

Warm mulches: Mulching is also a great option for keeping soil and plant roots warm. You can purchase mulch or make your own by adding things like leaves that have fallen from trees (disease free of course) or grass clippings and hay. Mulch helps to ensure that soil stays warm and is protected.

Harvesting Your Produce

Most produce loses about 30% of its nutrients within 72 hours of being picked. One of the biggest advantages of homesteading is that you don't have to worry about how far your food has to travel or how long it has been sitting in a grocery store. You can eat it right off of the vine if you want to. That is truly farm to table!

For example, eating spinach right when it has been picked saves you from losing 90% of its nutrient content. Not only do foods retain a higher nutritional content when you eat them shortly after being picked, but you are also ensuring optimal flavor and peak freshness.

Herbs are a great and easy option to start harvesting as many of them have a repeat yield. This simply means that once you have harvested herbs off of the plant, it will continue to grow and give you more fresh herbs.

Each type of produce that you grow will need to be harvested at different times depending on the maturity rate of the plant. It is better to pick produce at its peak ripeness if you are going to use it right away. Otherwise, in order to avoid waste and spoilage, you can pick produce a few days before you plan to use it even if it is not fully ripe. Then, just let it ripen off of the vine. Picking your fruits and vegetables on time can ensure the plants will continue to bare produce.

Fall Homesteading Activities

Fall is a very important time of year for homesteaders. There is a lot of work to be done on a homestead before winter starts, particularly if you live in colder weather areas where you tend to get a lot of snow. Fall activities can help to extend your growing season, clean up your homestead, prepare and prevent against pests and diseases, and ensure that your compost pile is thriving.

If you do not already have compost started, fall is a great time to start as you have access to plenty of leaves and other organic matter. Fall is also a great time for canning and preserving your harvest so that you have enough food over the winter months. If you are saving seeds, now is the time to prepare those seeds to make sure that they will be ready for the next growing season.

Instead of waiting for spring to declutter your homestead, why not do it in the fall? While you are cleaning out your crops and gardens, don't forget to also clean out your home, outbuildings, storage units, and barn. You should also make sure that any livestock you have on your homestead is adequately prepared for winter. This might include nesting boxes for your chickens or heated water bowls for your cattle. Fall is also a great time to do a perimeter check and see if there are any areas of fencing that need to be repaired.

Here is a list of things to check in order to make sure that your property is in tip-top shape:

- ☒ Repair fencing
- ☒ Outdoor lighting
- ☒ Outdoor electrical units
- ☒ Animals have adequate shelter
- ☒ Declutter storage areas
- ☒ Clean heat source
- ☒ Seal windows and doors
- ☒ Gather firewood
- ☒ Clean up garden/crops
- ☒ Clean off gardening tools
- ☒ Maintain tractor or other vehicles
- ☒ Put cold frames in place
- ☒ Stock up on feed
- ☒ Store outdoor furniture
- ☒ Maintenance generator
- ☒ Prune your trees

Chapter Summary

Once your harvest is planted, you will need to continually look after it so that it remains healthy and you get the highest crop yield possible from your efforts.

You should walk your garden on a regular basis, preferably daily, in order to pick weeds and assess the health of your plants. It is best to water your crops early in the morning as the ground is cooler and the water will be absorbed further into the soil. Crops should also be watered as close to the base of the plant as possible while avoiding getting the leaves wet.

You can also feed your crops through the use of fertilizers to add additional nutrients. How much fertilizer you add to your soil depends on what type of plants you are feeding. For example, crops like broccoli and kale need more fertilizer than arugula and peas.

Pruning and thinning your plants is also vital to the health of your crops. This allows parts of the plant that are not beneficial to be trimmed away. It also helps to allow more sunlight through shrubs and trees to reach vital parts of the plant.

Crops can also be planted next to one another as a way to support each other. This support might come from the physical support used by vining plants or another plant providing additional nutrients. It is advised with vining plants that you use some type of support structure to help save space within your garden. Support structures can either be purchased or made out of scrap wood.

You will need to make sure that you are able to manage weeds within your crops as they will compete for the nutrients in the soil. Mulching is a great way to help prevent additional weed growth and offers other benefits to the soil, such as insulation.

If you are experiencing pest or disease problems, you will first need to determine what you are dealing with and then come up with a solution to save your crops. Monitoring the weather conditions can help prevent the spread of disease and pests; as well as give homesteaders insights into how to protect their plants.

Even if the weather does not cooperate, you can find ways to extend your growing season. This might include growing inside of a greenhouse, using various forms of plant protectors, or by placing mulch over the soil.

When it comes to harvesting your produce, it is best to harvest it as close to the time you are going to eat it as you can. Many fruits and vegetables lose a lot of their nutrient content after being picked. While plants like herbs can be picked and will continually produce, plants like spinach lose up to 90% of their nutritional value within the first 24 hours of being picked.

Lastly, there are many activities that you can do on your homestead during the fall to ensure that you can self-sustain over the winter. From winterizing at your bees to cleaning off your gardening tools, being prepared for winter is very important on a homestead.

In the next chapter, we will focus on all of the different plant varieties.

CHAPTER FIVE
Individual Plants

THIS CHAPTER WILL help you select appropriate plants based on the conditions of your land while understanding the practices you will have to use to successfully plant, grow, and harvest particular crops.

We will cover the different categories of plants, the differences between warm-season and cold-season vegetables, the different types of fruit plants, and the best crops to grow in shade as well as urban areas. We will also cover how things like hardiness can affect the growing timeline and the requirements and activities for individual plants.

Plant Categories

There are many ways to classify plants. One way is to group them into four different categories: non-vascular and vascular plants, gymnosperms, and angiosperms.

Non-vascular: Lack a vascular tissue system to transport water or nutrients (moss).

Vascular: Possess a vascular system through which they can transport water and nutrients (fern).

Gymnosperms: Possess a vascular system and bear wood and green needle-like or scale-like foliage (pine trees).

Angiosperms: Flowering plants with a vascular system that produce their reproductive organs within a flower (pretty much everything that you would grow).

Top level plant categories

Within the Angiosperm classification of plants, there are vegetables, fruits, herbs, and flowers. Fruits are pretty easy to classify as they are anything that contains a seed (yes, this includes tomatoes). Herbs are much smaller plants and are classified as having aromatic and savory properties and do not contain large amounts of macronutrients. They are used for medicinal purposes and to flavor or garnish food.

Edible flowers are a fun crop to grow as they add color to your garden and your plate. Edible flowers can be sprinkled into salads, baked into breads or cakes, candied and used as a garnish, dried and used for herbal teas, and even incorporated into a cocktail.

Vegetables are the most commonly grown crops on homesteads, other than tomatoes. Speaking in technical terms, a fruit is the part of the plant that bears seeds. Vegetables, however, are the roots (carrots), leaves (kale), stems (celery), and any other parts of the plant that you might eat.

Cold- season verses warm-season vegetables

Knowing the differences between your warm-season and cold-season vegetables can mean the difference between a fruitful harvest and a harvest that is lacking. Your cold-season crops are the ones that you plant first thing in the spring before the last frost date. Cold-season plants can withstand colder temperatures and also need the cold in order to start germinating and maturing. Some of the most resilient cold-season vegetables will even need a bit of frost to reach their full potential.

Cold-season crops should also be harvested before it gets too warm outside. They should be planted early enough in the season so that they can fully mature before the weather warms up. If they grow too long in the hot weather their quality can greatly diminish. Additionally, cold-season vegetables are generally grown directly from seeds sown into the ground, rather than from seedlings, as soon as the soil is soft enough to work with.

Warm-season crops require higher temperatures, both in the soil and in the air, and are always planted after the last frost so as not to damage the plants. Warm-season crops are generally started indoors and then transplanted as soon as it is warm enough outside. This is beneficial since some warm-season crops, such as watermelons, take longer to mature; however, starting warm-season crops indoors and then transferring them will give you a jump start on the growing season. Additionally, warm-season vegetables only have one growing cycle, whereas cold-season vegetables can have more than one.

Fruit-bearing Plants

There are different types of fruit-bearing plants: vining plants, ground cover plants, bushes, brambles, and trees. While fruit-bearing plants can be found all of these categories of plants, not all plants in these categories can bear fruit.

Best Crops for Urban Farming

If you would like to try your hand at growing your own food before you get a homestead, then you might want to consider urban farming. The great thing about urban farming is that pretty much anything that you can grow in a container; you can grow in your home. Urban farming is also great because you are often farming indoors, which means you can have access to your harvest all year round.

For larger plants, you can get dwarf varieties that will do better inside of your home. You can also regrow food from kitchen scraps; talk about upcycling! When you are regrowing food from kitchen scraps, make sure that you are using high-quality sources. These can be organic vegetables that you have purchased from the grocery store or organic vegetables that you have purchased directly from a farmer or through a CSA program. Here are just a handful of things that you can grow in your urban garden either from seed or from kitchen scraps:

- ☒ Green onions
- ☒ Celery
- ☒ Romaine lettuce, bok choy, cabbage
- ☒ Carrots
- ☒ Leeks
- ☒ Onions
- ☒ Harbs
- ☒ Pineapple
- ☒ Potatoes
- ☒ Sweet potatoes

Plants that do well in shade

While you can grow a bounty of food inside of your home, there might not always be adequate lighting to grow every kind of plant. In that case, you should choose plants that do well in the shade. These can include:

- ☒ Chives
- ☒ Oregano
- ☒ Parsley
- ☒ Tarragon
- ☒ Cilantro
- ☒ Lemon balm
- ☒ Mint

Be careful with mint though; keep it separated as it can often overtake a container.

Short-season crops

Short-season crops are great if you are planting early and want to plant two yields or more of the same vegetable. They are also optimal for when you live in an area that might have a shorter growing season, such as the Pacific Northwest. Not to mention that you could be eating your harvest a lot sooner too!

Here are a handful of short-season vegetables that you can grow in two months or less:

- ☒ Snap peas
- ☒ Beets
- ☒ Broccoli
- ☒ Cucumbers
- ☒ Green onions
- ☒ Kale

- ☒ Bok Choy
- ☒ Lettuce
- ☒ Okra
- ☒ Radishes
- ☒ Spinach
- ☒ Summer squash

How Hardiness Can Affect Growing Timelines

As the climate and the weather changes, farmers and homesteaders need to be more aware of temperature and how it can affect your crops. Keep a log of what you are planting and when, and the outcomes of each. This can help you to make more informed decisions in subsequent years.

Changes in the climate have also affected the temperature; annuals that would normally stop growing in September might last all the way through November. You will need to be able to track the temperature as well as keep records of certain seasonal changes that might affect your crops and overall yield.

Chapter Summary

As a homesteader, you learn a lot about the science of plants and how they can work with one another. You also become very aware of the different categories of plants and how to effectively utilize each of those categories.

Knowing the difference between warm-season crops and cold-season crops can mean the difference between a significant crop yield and an insignificant one. While cold weather crops should be harvested before the weather gets too warm, you can plant them multiple times which results in an overall higher yield. Warm-season crops, on the other hand, take longer to reach their full maturity and will only result in one yield before the season ends.

If you would like to try your hand at urban farming before you jump into homesteading, there are many plants that do very well indoors, in containers, and in low-light situations. In addition, you can also experiment with growing your own produce from kitchen scraps.

Homesteaders can also benefit from short-season crops, as there is less time between planting and getting the produce on your plate. This is also good for areas that do not have a very long growing season as some vegetables can be grown and harvested in as little as two months.

In the next chapter, we will focus on upping your level of self-sufficiency by adding livestock to your homestead. Whether you have a quarter of an acre or several hundred acres, there are various options when it comes to incorporating livestock.

CHAPTER SIX
Livestock

ADDING LIVESTOCK TO your homestead can increase your self-sufficiency as well as create an additional stream of income. Having your own livestock can give you a steady supply of meat, milk, and eggs. Additionally, raising your own animals means that you can raise them free of hormones and other chemicals and process them in ethical and humane ways.

Even a rather small homestead, about one-quarter acre, can support some types of livestock. Depending on which types of animals that you are planning to raise will determine how much space you will need for storage and pasture. The most common types of livestock to have are: cows, goats, poultry (chicken, ducks, turkeys, etc), pigs, and rabbits.

When you add livestock to your homestead, you can breed and sell the animals as well as the products and byproducts derived from them. In this chapter, we will discuss which types of livestock you should add to your homestead, what you can do with that livestock, humane and ethical processing practices and, while not traditionally considered livestock, a bit about beekeeping.

What Types of Livestock to Raise

The main types of livestock to raise include:

- Milking cows
- Beef cows
- Calves
- Rabbits
- Chickens
- Ducks
- Turkey
- Goats
- Sheep
- Hogs/Pigs

In addition to the above, you can also have dogs and cats on your homestead. Dogs are great for providing protection, security, companionship, and they can even help with herding.

Products and Byproducts

When you are raising livestock, you have direct access to animal products and byproducts that will greatly benefit your family, and that you can also use and sell for a profit. Each type of livestock has its own level of importance, and when used properly, can be very beneficial to your homestead.

Cows

There are many different varieties of cows available, but the two basic categories are milk cows, and beef cows. Milk cows, obviously, produce milk. This milk can be sold as is or made into cheese, buttermilk, butter, fresh yogurt, or different types of creams. High quality, hormone-free milk products also sell really well. I personally have paid $9 for a gallon of raw milk before I was a homesteader. Just be sure to check with your local ordinances because in some areas it is illegal to sell raw milk or raw milk products. Additionally, all cows are not created equal. Make sure to do your research and talk with other homesteaders who keep dairy cows before going out and purchasing one.

You can also raise beef cows on your homestead that you can eventually slaughter and either sell the meat or use it to feed your family. If you are planning on selling it, you can command decent prices for high-quality grass-fed meats of any kind. For colder temperatures, Scottish Highland cows are great for meat, milk production, and foraging. They also birth easy, which is important.

Cows will need a good amount of room to graze, approximately one acre. However, a minimum of two acres is even better so that you can rotate the pasture. Not to mention, cows can form a sort of symbiotic relationship with the trees on your land. Trees can provide the cow with shade while the cow provides fertilizer. Not to mention, cows make a great replacement for a lawnmower. A milk cow can produce on average about six gallons of milk per day. So unless you are making a lot of milk products that freeze well, you might want to consider selling or sharing your cow byproducts. Furthermore, a full size 1200 pound cow will yield about 750 pounds of meat, and at $5 to $9 per pound, that can be a pretty good source of income.

Poultry

Any type of poultry, particularly chickens, is great to have on a homestead. Other than providing eggs and meat, chickens are friendly creatures that will enjoy socializing with other animals on your homestead. Also, chickens are some of the easiest livestock to care for.

One of the chicken byproducts that people might not normally consider using is feathers. After feathers have been dried and cleaned, they can be used for pillow stuffing or feather mattresses. You can also use them to make feather dusters or to decorate handmade items, using rooster feathers in hats or flower arrangements.

Another byproduct, chicken manure, is great to add to compost as it has a very high nitrogen compound and will help your produce thrive. Additionally, homesteaders can raise more than just chickens; they might also have ducks, geese, turkeys, and guinea fowl. All of which are excellent sources of meat, eggs, and feathers. Duck eggs, which can be more difficult to come by, can be sold for much higher prices and are especially good for you. Guinea fowl are great at managing pests and can even be used in place of watchdogs.

Goats, sheep, lambs

If you want to reap the benefits of milk but don't have room for a cow, a goat is your next best option. Goats are fairly easy to care for and are self-reliant; however, they can be rather crafty and might require some strong fencing to keep them contained. Goats are also great if you want the benefit of having milk without having to worry about making too much, as dairy goats only produce about two to four quarts per day (that is about one half gallon to one gallon), which is much more manageable than six gallons. Goat milk can be sold as is or used for making goat milk soap, butter, and cheese.

Goats can also be used for other byproducts, such as long-haired goats being used for their coats. The most commonly used goats for this are Angora goats, which when sheared, produce fiber that you can either sell or use to make beautifully handcrafted products. You may also choose to butcher goats for their meat, which has a unique flavor and is also very healthy.

Goats can also be used around your homestead as your own personal clean-up crew. They love to eat things like junk, trees, bushes, weeds, and other plant byproducts. Just as with other types of livestock, the milk and meat that comes from goats and cows is directly affected by what they consume. Additionally, if you also have horses or mules, grazing a goat with an unbroken, larger animal can be effective in helping to train them. When larger animals see the goats interacting with you and getting food from you this also helps to build trust with them.

Sheep can be used for their wool, milk, and meat. When sheep graze and eat grass, they produce a really great fertilizer for your plants and homestead. You also never have to worry about buying grain for your sheep as they are 100% grass-fed. Sheep, much like goats, are great for smaller acre plots of land. Sheep are also not as crafty as goats and are the easiest animals to handle.

Lambs, or young sheep, can be butchered for the production of veal.

Pigs and hogs

Pigs and hogs are great animals to add to your homestead. You can get approximately 144 pounds of meat from a 250-pound hog which can be used to either feed your family or to sell. Hogs and pigs also don't require as much space as other animals do, are great for forging, and make great companions for dogs. Similar to the relationship between cows and trees, hogs can also have a symbiotic relationship with your garden by eating weeds and leftover veggies while adding to your compost.

Hogs and pigs are also built-in garbage disposals. Anything that you don't feed to your dogs or chickens can go directly to a pig as they eat just about anything and everything. People often view pigs as dirty animals when they are actually rather clean. Pigs, similar to cows, really enjoy being able to free-range in a pasture. However, pigs also need pretty strong pens since they are strong and can get out if they really want to.

Rabbits

Rabbits are an easy animal to care for and adorable addition to your homestead. Rabbits take up very little space and don't cost a lot to feed, plus they can also make a great additional source of meat. Rabbits are also easy to breed and their gestation periods are very short, so you can produce a lot of rabbits very quickly. Rabbits will eat most veggies and veggie scraps and can produce a great fertilizer for your garden. You can easily purchase or build hutches for your rabbits or let them free range in an area of your pasture. Just make sure that they also have somewhere to stay when it is too cold outside.

One thing that I would like to mention about the animals that we have discussed here is that they are all very smart. Cows can learn to open their own pens, chickens can purr just like cats, and goats can intelligently escape just about any type of fencing you put them in. So make sure that you are treating your animals well, and they will certainly repay you for it.

Butchering and Processing Meat

Each type of animal requires a different butchering process. Smaller animals like chickens and rabbits are fairly simple and can be butchered right on your homestead, while, if you are not experienced, you might want to take your larger animals to be processed. This way, you are getting the best cuts of meat. Also, try to use as much of the animal as possible with little waste.

For example, chicken feathers can be used for crafts, or filling pillows. You can use the head, feet, and any remaining bones to make chicken stock. This is filled with collagen which is great for your skin.

Rabbits, although small, breed and grow quickly and can produce hundreds of pounds of meat a year. Without getting into detail specifically on how to butcher each of the animals, just know that it can take some time before you become accustomed to butchering your own animals on your homestead. A rabbit is butchered much like a chicken in that you can get breast and thigh pieces. Rabbit pelts can also be used to make blankets, hats, and other sorts of clothing. Other parts of the animal, such as the ears, brain, or blood, can be used as feed for other animals, including dogs.

Pigs, goats, sheep, and cows can also be used for meat. However, this process is also much more time-intensive and requires a lot more knowledge to complete correctly. If you are not ready to take on this task, then you should take your meat to a butcher to be processed. As with smaller animals, try and use every part of the animal as your pioneer ancestors would have. Bones from any animal can be made into amazing bone broth, which is a health tonic all on its own.

Beekeeping

Bees are a great addition to any homestead, especially considering the decline of bees in the world. Bees don't require a lot of maintenance, but they do require a little more equipment to get started. However, you can always get started with a minimalist setup and grow it over time. You will need a hive box, a source of water, and a beekeeping suit to get started. You don't even have to actually buy the bees; you can simply catch them in the spring with some sugar water.

Contrary to what people might think, bees are not difficult to keep, nor are they vicious. However, I would not suggest keeping them in a high traffic area on your property. Bees serve your homestead well and have several benefits, including providing you with honey, beeswax, and propolis. While there is a lot to learn with beekeeping, there are also many benefits to keeping bees.

Raw local honey can bring in a good income and is a great staple for any homestead. You can also separate and use the beeswax for a number of different things, like making candles, lip gloss, and preserving any cheese that you make.

Chapter Summary

Adding livestock to your homestead gives you an additional stream of income as well as increases your overall self-sufficiency. Even smaller homesteads can support some type of livestock. The livestock you choose depends on which products and byproducts you are looking to produce, as well as the amount of land you have available. Some of the most common types of livestock for homesteads include cows, rabbits, chickens, and goats.

Raising livestock can help you produce direct byproducts, such as meat and milk. In addition, there are also many other byproducts that you can produce from livestock on your homestead. Adding livestock to your homestead also creates a symbiotic relationship with the fruits and vegetables that you are producing. Your animals can be given part of your produce as feed and then, in turn, will help to fertilize your growing efforts.

While many homesteaders choose to butcher and process their own animals, you need to ensure that you are knowledgeable on the process so it is done correctly. Of course, you can always take your animals to a butcher to be processed if you are not comfortable doing it yourself.

CHAPTER SEVEN
Food Preservation and Storage

N O MATTER HOW big or small of a homestead you have, you will need to preserve and store some of the food that you harvest. During the off season, in order to keep food from spoiling, homesteaders need a strategy and process for preserving their harvest throughout the winter.

This chapter will look at the most common methods used to preserve food which include canning, drying, freezing, fermenting, leaving food in the ground, and seed saving.

Canning

Canning is probably one of the most well-known methods of food preservation for homesteaders. Canning includes water bath canning and pressure canning, as well as hot packing and raw packing. While the methods and processes for canning are simple, you do need to know what you're doing in order to avoid any potential disasters, such as busted mason jars or botulism.

Water bath canning

Water bath canning is great for foods that are higher in acidity, such as fruits and jams, tomatoes, pickles, vinegar, and other condiments. You can easily do water bath canning with a few simple tools, such as a large deep pot with a lid and rack. There are also many inexpensive water bath canning kits available. In order to properly preserve produce with water bath canning, you need to ensure that the jars are upright and fully submerged in the water bath.

In order to ensure the safety of your food preservation, make sure that all parts of the glass jars and lids are properly sanitized in hot soapy water and thoroughly dried. Prevent the jars from cracking by preheating them before filling them with hot food. You can ensure that the jars have been properly sealed when you can remove the outer ring from the lid without the jar opening. Many homesteaders remove the rings from the jars before storing them. Additionally, make sure that there is no food residue left when the outer ring is removed by wiping down the jar with a clean damp cloth.

Pressure canning

Pressure canning is great for low-acid foods, including most vegetables, poultry, meats, and seafood. Canning allows food to be processed at a much higher temperature (240 °F) in order to prevent spoilage. When combining both high and low acidity foods, it is best to can them as you would low acidity food.

One of the commonalities between water bath canning and pressure canning is that all of the jars need to have room for headspace when they are being prepared. You should also ensure that all of the jars and lids have been properly sanitized. This will help to prevent any food spoilage and keep your food for longer periods of time. You should also check to make sure that all of the jars, lids, and bands that you are using are in proper working order and there are no dents or nicks. Similar to the water bath canning method, anything that is canned with a pressure cooker should also be preheated. This will prevent the jars from breaking when they are filled with hot food.

While the pressure canner also requires water, it is minimal compared to the water bath canning method. While they may seem intimidating, pressure canners are actually very easy to use. Simply follow the directions the pressure canner and always ensure that the canner is undisturbed after the canning process is complete and pressure returns to zero. This will ensure that all of the pressure is out of the pressure canner and that you will not have any mishaps. Once you remove the cans from the pressure canner, set the alarm on a towel in an upright position and leave the cans undisturbed for 24 hours. Do not fuss with trying to tighten the lids or move around the contents.

Hot pack and cold pack canning

When you are preparing your food to be canned there are two different methods: cold pack and hot pack canning. When you use the cold pack canning method, you put freshly prepared and unheated food into your mason jars. The food itself remains raw, but the jars need to be hot and the liquid that goes inside of them needs to be brought to a boil before it is added. Cold pack canning is often done by using a pressure canner. Hot pack canning, however, entails boiling freshly prepared foods. Once the foods are prepared and cooked, the jars are filled with the hot food or liquid. The hot pack canning method is generally used with a water bath canner. The process of hot pack canning helps to remove more air from the food which also allows you to get more food in a single can and improves the overall shelf life of its contents.

One of the biggest benefits of preserving your food through canning is that it drastically extends your harvest. Canned foods can last from one to two years, sometimes even longer. Although canning can be advantageous, foods do not retain the same nutrient content nor will they taste the same as fresh produce. Glass jars can easily break, broken seals can cause spoilage, and the entire process of canning can be time-consuming. When canned foods become spoiled they can be dangerous to your health.

Safety precautions

One of the most common reasons that people avoid canning foods is due to a foodborne toxin known as botulism. Botulism is a deadly toxin that you cannot see, taste, or smell. Oftentimes, foods contaminated with botulism were either prepared by not following proper canning instructions, canned without the use of a pressure canner, or canned even though they had previously shown signs of spoilage. For canned foods such as tomatoes, you can boil them in a saucepan before consuming them. Make sure that you are also storing canned or pickled foods in a refrigerator after the cans have been opened.

You can determine when and which canning methods to use by knowing the acidity of the food that you are preserving. Foods that are less acidic (less than 4.6pH) should be canned with a pressure canner. Foods with higher acidity (more than 4.6pH) should use the water canning method.

There are many advantages to canning. If you choose to pickle your food before canning it you can easily add unique flavors to your meals that might otherwise have been bland. Pickled and fermented foods also have higher nutrient density than those that are frozen or dehydrated.

Drying Fruits and Vegetables

The two most common methods you can use to dry your fruits and vegetables are: dehydration and freeze-drying. Fruits and vegetables that have been dried are nutritious, lighter, easier to store, and are very tasty. It is also much less time consuming to dry or freeze-dry food. Simply prepare your fruits and vegetables, place them in your dehydrator or freeze dryer, and then bag them up and label them.

Foods that have been dried or freeze-dried make great high energy snacks as well as quick and healthy snacks that you can eat anywhere, even while working on your homestead. While a freeze dryer is certainly an investment, it can preserve food for YEARS! You can make and freeze-dry meals and rehydrate them when you are going to eat them.

Some of the most ideal foods to freeze and rehydrate include:

- Apples
- Pears
- Peaches
- Bananas
- Plums
- Cantaloupe
- Avocados
- Strawberries
- Blueberries
- Carrots
- Corn
- Celery
- Potato
- Green beans
- Tomato
- Mangos

You can also transform various types of fruits into fruit leathers and rolls. Meats can be prepared and dried as jerky, and herbs are one of the easiest things to dry in a dehydrator.

The processes of dehydrating and freeze-drying are very similar. They both work to remove the moisture out of food while retaining the nutrients and increasing the flavor. Food can be dried either in a dehydrator, an oven, or in a freeze-dryer. Dehydrators work by moving warm air around the food to draw out the moisture. You can dry food in an oven by maintaining a low temperature which then uses heat from the oven to draw out the moisture of the produce. Freeze-dryers first freeze the food and then use a dehydration process to remove the moisture.

The process of drying fruits and vegetables through dehydration or freeze-drying helps to remove all of the moisture from the plant. This helps to eliminate the growth of microorganisms which prevents food spoilage. Dehydrating and freeze-drying fruits and vegetables also helps to maintain valuable enzymes. Specifically, if foods are dehydrated 117°F or less, all of the enzymes are preserved.

Foods that have been processed using dehydration and freeze-drying methods are also very easy to store. Once fully dried you can store them in Mylar or zip lock plastic bags and they will keep for up to two years (even longer for freeze dried foods).

Freezing

Freezing your food is one of the many preservation processes that help to delay spoilage. The process of freezing food for preservation as a common method dates all the way back to the early 1900s. In prehistoric times, people would use ice and snow in an attempt to preserve the animals that they hunted.

When you freeze your food it delays spoilage. Freezing food is effective for deterring many micro-organisms; however, it does not deter the growth of parasites. Some people might say that freezing destroys many of the nutrients within the food but this is simply not true. The process of freezing has very little effect on the nutrient content of produce and other foods.

The most effective way to preserve fruits and vegetables when freezing them is to first wash them, blanch them, thoroughly dry them, and then package them in airtight containers. This process works particularly well for young vegetables.

You can preserve the nutrient content of food by first blanching it. This means that it is submerged in boiling water, and then submerged in ice water to stop the cooking process. Freezing your food allows you to save more of your bounty while retaining a good amount of the nutrients. You also don't have to worry about any preservatives being added when you are doing your own freezing.

Fermenting

Fermenting food is an ancient process of food preservation. Many commercial producers still use the same fermentation methods today to make things like cheese, wine, sauerkraut, and yogurt. Fermented foods are great because they are packed with beneficial probiotics. They also help build a strong immune system and aide in better digestion.

The process of fermenting food takes a little more knowledge than either freezing or dehydrating since you need to be aware of the safety measures. Fermenting is worth the extra effort though and adds a whole host of health benefits to your daily diet.

The process of fermentation makes food even healthier than when it is in its raw form. Adding fermented foods to your diet can drastically improve your gut health and can help defend against common illnesses. The process of fermentation also breaks down enzymes in food, making it easier to digest. This can also help to promote weight loss.

While many people benefit from eating fermented foods, others might experience some negative side effects, like bloating, due to its high probiotic content. When you are first fermenting food, make sure that you are paying close attention to the directions and are following each and every step. Knowing what you are doing helps prevent any potential health hazards or exploding bottles (not that I would know from experience). If your equipment is not properly sanitized your food can spoil, making it unsafe to consume. However, this is easily preventable with proper sanitation and preparation.

Some of the foods that you can make with common fermentation practices are:

- ☒ Kefir (water or milk)
- ☒ Sauerkraut
- ☒ Tempeh
- ☒ Natto
- ☒ Cheeses
- ☒ Kombucha (fermented tea)
- ☒ Miso
- ☒ Kimchi (cabbage and peppers)
- ☒ Salami
- ☒ Yogurt
- ☒ Sourdough bread
- ☒ Beer
- ☒ Wine

Two different fermentation processes that you can use are fermenting or pickling (also known as brining). With fermenting, fermented foods feed off of themselves as well as the sugars that they produce in order to further the fermentation process. Pickling, however, uses a salty or acidic brine to preserve the food. You can either go high tech with your fermentation process or do it the old school way by using ceramic crocks.

Leaving in the Ground

You can also leave certain vegetables in the ground for longer periods of time to preserve them. Turnips, in particular, can be left in the ground until you need to use them, even in the middle of winter. Vegetables that are left in the ground over winter should be covered with straw, hay, or mulch in order to prevent them from freezing and to also preserve the quality of the plants. Some crops that work well with this method are:

- ☒ Cabbage
- ☒ Beets
- ☒ Carrots
- ☒ Parsnips
- ☒ Turnips

Seed Saving

Saving seeds is another ancient practice used by homesteaders. It is best to save seeds that are self-pollinating and require little to no special treatment before saving. This can include tomatoes and peppers (which are both technically fruits), beans, and peas. Other plants need two growing seasons to set seed, which can make seed saving a bit more difficult. This mainly applies to biennial crops, such as beets and carrots.

In order to save seeds, you need to harvest your produce at the ideal time and store the seeds correctly over the winter. There are four different kinds of pollination methods that plants use to create more plants:

self-pollination, cross-pollination, open-pollination, and hybrid.

Saving seeds from self-pollinating plants is by far the easiest method. These plants produce seeds that need very little treatment before saving. Some of the easiest self-pollinating seeds to collect are from zucchini, pepper plants, tomatoes, and most types of fruit.

Cross-pollinating plants require a little more preparation and need a male and a female flower to produce more plants. These plants include corn and other vine crops. Cross-pollinating plants can easily mix seed strands with one another. For example, various strands of corn can cross-pollinate if they are planted too close to each other or their seed is spread by the wind. It is also common for insects to cross-pollinate crops like cucumbers and melons.

While current crops are not affected by cross-pollination, subsequent crops will be. Cross-pollination of crops can result in seeds that are impure and produce crops that are not very flavorful or as nutritious.

Other than self-pollinating plants, the second best option is open-pollinating plants. Open-pollinating varieties can easily set seed which results in the same variety of plants that are of higher quality. Heirloom varieties often come from open-pollinating plants and these seeds can be passed down through generations. There are a few things that you need to do when you start planting open-pollinating plants such as:

- ☒ Choose the best plants to save seed from.
- ☒ Choose the fastest growing and best-tasting plants.
- ☒ Never save seed from off-type or weak plants.

Finally, there are the hybrid varieties. Hybrids come from a cross between two different plant varieties, like two parents coming together to produce a beautiful child. Hybrid plants are bred to resist disease, be productive, and have outstanding vigor.

There are several characteristics of hybrid plants that classify them as hybrids:

- ☒ Plants that are grown from hybrid seeds will not match the parent plants but retain some of the characteristics.
- ☒ Hybrids will produce a new combination and can incorporate both good and bad traits of the parent plants.
- ☒ Creating a hybrid is a bit of a gamble, you never quite know what you will end up with.

How to Store Your Harvest

You can easily store certain types of produce without having to put it through preservation methods. Here are some of the best methods for storing, developed by centuries of homesteaders:

- ☒ Wrap apples and pears in newspaper and place them in a single layer inside the bottom of a container in your root cellar.
- ☒ For root vegetables, cut off any leafy tops and lay them in a single layer without any wrapping. Cover them with a layer of sand to prevent them from becoming rubbery. This is similar to leaving them in the ground.
- ☒ Upon harvesting your potatoes, leave them out in the sun to dry, remove any mud or dirt, and store them in paper sacks. Potatoes and other root vegetables do well when stored in a root cellar.
- ☒ You can leave parsnips in the ground and harvest them when you need them.
- ☒ For onions, garlic, and shallots, cut the tops off, and then place them inside clean pantyhose, tying a knot between each one. Then store them in a cool, dry place.
- ☒ Once picked, zucchini can be kept in cold storage for a few weeks.
- ☒ Squash and pumpkins can be kept in a cool, dry place for months.
- ☒ Leafy crops do best when they are eaten as close to being harvested as possible. You can extend your harvest into early winter by staggering your planting.
- ☒ Any kind of legumes, peas, or beans can be dried and then stored, blanched and frozen, or canned for preservation.

Chapter Summary

After you have harvested your crops you will need to ensure that you are properly preserving and storing your food so that you can maximize your harvest. There are several methods that a homesteader uses for food preservation which includes canning, dehydrating, freeze-drying, freezing, fermenting, and pickling. Homesteaders also choose to save seeds as a way to continue their harvest in subsequent years.

With any food preservation method, you should ensure that you have all of the proper equipment before you begin and are knowledgeable in proper preparation and sanitation methods. Foods that are lower in acidity should be canned with the use of a pressure canner, whereas high acidity foods should be canned by using the water canning method.

Food storage methods are also important. Canned foods can be stored in a cool dry place, dried and freeze-dried foods can be stored in airtight containers, while other foods like fresh apples and carrots can be stored in a root cellar. Make sure that you also have all of your storage areas ready to go before proceeding with your food preservation.

In the next chapter, we are going to discuss how homesteaders can profit from their land.

CHAPTER EIGHT
Profiting From Your Land

FROM PURCHASING LIVESTOCK to purchasing large pieces of equipment, starting and maintaining a homestead can become very expensive. In order to offset some of those costs and create extra income, some homesteaders choose to sell products that are made from things they produce on their land.

With some proper planning and a lot of elbow grease, there are many different ways to make money homesteading. If you are already producing things on your homestead, why not produce a little extra and make some money from it in order to help financially sustain your homestead. You can make money as a homesteader by selling vegetables and other produce, teaching a homesteading course, or renting out some of the equipment that you have already purchased.

What to Sell

While most people think of selling vegetables at a farmers market as one of the only ways that you can make money homesteading, there are actually many different ways in which you can create additional income.

Produce

Produce can include everything from vegetables, herbs, mushrooms, and fruits. You can sell these items at a local farmers market or craft fair. You can also sell items directly out of your homestead, or through a local CSA (community-supported agriculture). You can produce food specifically for this purpose or by using leftover produce that your family does not consume or preserve. You might also consider donating any surplus produce to a local food pantry to help those in need. While not an income, any donations that you make are considered tax-deductible.

Fresh cut flowers, while not edible produce, are also a great way to make a few extra dollars. Just like traditional produce, you can sell flowers at a farmers market or craft fair, or you can partner with local shops and supply them directly with flowers. Other produce, such as fresh or dried traditional and medicinal herbs, can also be sold. Herbs are a great source of income since they don't cost a lot to get started. You can also sell them for a pretty high return-on-investment, particularly if you are able to produce some that are uncommon to that area.

Classes

People are becoming increasingly interested in homesteading. Teaching classes gives you an opportunity to share your knowledge, connect with other like-minded individuals, as well as create a good source of additional income. Depending on what you have available on your property and the knowledge that you have, you can create courses in any area of homesteading. This can include gardening, beekeeping, equine care, livestock, foraging, and even things like soap making. You can advertise your classes independently or you can partner with other organizations, such as departments, schools, or churches.

You can also hold your classes either in person or virtually. One of the biggest advantages of holding in-person classes, other than meeting new people, is that you got a group of people to help you with your homesteading responsibilities. This helps to take some of the physical load off of you while providing your students with hands-on experience. You can also provide the same classes virtually, either as an independent provider or through course platforms. One of the biggest advantages of providing virtual classes is that you only have to teach the class one time and people can continually buy it. This provides you with a source of passive income and it doesn't take you more time to teach the course over and over again.

Blogging, YouTube, and Freelancing

Similar to holding virtual classes, you can also create additional income from your homestead by blogging about it, creating YouTube videos, or offering freelance services. Freelancing can include writing about various homesteading topics for other blogs or websites. Creating your own blog, however, is a great way to share your knowledge and experience and will give you much more control over the creative process. YouTube videos are great if you like to be on camera and want to show the various processes of homesteading rather than just writing about them.

As more and more people become interested in homesteading, the research topics based around homesteading continues to increase. This makes it easy for those who want to start a blog, YouTube channel, or begin freelance writing, to create content around various homesteading topics. There are many people who are making a very good income working online by blogging, working with YouTube, and offering their freelance services. Oftentimes, homesteaders are able to replace their full-time jobs and start working less in order to spend more time staying home and raising their families.

One of the biggest advantages of working virtually as a blogger, YouTuber, or freelancer is that it is fairly easy to get started. While there is a bit of a learning curve, if you are passionate about homesteading and want to share your knowledge with others, it is a great way to start. You don't even have to be a great writer or be a natural on camera to provide value to your audience.

Handmade crafts and gifts

Many of the things found or produced on a homestead can be used to make artisan products such as goat milk soap, feed bag totes, and plant markers. Take a look at the things in and around your homestead. For example, feed bags can be upcycled and transformed into stylish tote bags. Not only are handmade crafts and gifts a great creative outlet, you can also make a great income from them by setting up a tent at a farmers market, or partnering with other local businesses and organizations. Some areas even have stores dedicated to Artisan and local products.

You can also sell handmade crafts and gifts online through your own website or through various platforms, one of the most popular being Etsy. On Etsy, you can sell anything that is handmade, digital, or vintage.

When coming up with ideas for different products to sell, look around at your homestead and the things that you currently use. This can include things like handmade plant markers, hearts, or even aprons with cute or funny sayings on them. If you are not a natural creative you can even turn to Pinterest for a wide variety of ideas that also include tutorials. To get you started, here is a list of various handmade crafts and gifts that you can produce and start selling from your homestead:

- ☒ Plant markers
- ☒ Tote bags upcycled from feed bags
- ☒ Upcycled clothing
- ☒ Fabric dyed with natural dyes such as beet juice
- ☒ Beeswax or other products from beekeeping
- ☒ Rabbit pelts
- ☒ Sheepskin
- ☒ Wool
- ☒ Christmas wreaths
- ☒ Homemade wood signs
- ☒ Pallet furniture
- ☒ Maple syrup
- ☒ Christmas trees

Livestock

If you have livestock on your homestead, you might want to consider selling some of it as a form of income. The livestock you sell can include any type of animal that is normally found on a homestead, mature or young, such as milk or beef cows, pigs, goats, rabbits, chickens, and even ducks. If you have a means of continually producing young livestock, such as through the use of a rooster, you might consider incubating fertile chicken eggs and selling them, rather than selling the chicks themselves.

You might also consider selling various byproducts of your livestock. These would be things like farm fresh eggs, milk, and fertile hatching eggs.

Specialty products

There are a lot of things that can fall under the category of specialty products. These products can even include mushrooms and foraged goods. Just make sure that you are knowledgeable about the items you are selling and provide as much information as possible to your customers.

Passive Income and Multiple Income Streams

I advise anyone that I work with to do two things when it comes to their finances. This includes setting up passive income as well as having multiple streams of income. It can take a while to set up both of these and both are something that you should continually work on. Passive income refers to any money that is made from something you do once that requires minimal effort to maintain. Having multiple income streams simply means having more than one way to make money.

Whether or not you live on a homestead, having both types of income streams is incredibly important. You never want to have to rely on just one stream of income because if that one stream stops, it can result in a downward spiral of negative consequences. However, if you have multiple streams of income and one stream stops, you will still have others that you can rely on. With active income, you only have so many hours in a day to earn money. When you are only generating income when you are actively working, you will never truly be financially free. Generating passive income allows you to still generate an income while working on other things.

Here is a little snapshot of how you can create both passive and multiple income streams from your homestead. Perhaps you have created an online course that you are able to continually sell while providing minimal updates and customer service. In addition to the money that you are making from your course, every Saturday you go to the farmers market and sell a variety of products. Then, in addition to the farmer's market, you are also partnering with local stores that sell your handmade soaps for you. In a scenario like this, you are checking the boxes for both passive and multiple income streams.

Lastly, make sure you are doing activities on your homestead that you enjoy making money from. If you hate writing, don't start a blog. If you are passionate about something and you find it fun, it is going to be easier for you to do it for longer periods of time.

Chapter Summary

As with any big venture, homesteading can be expensive. You can help offset some of the costs of running your homestead by selling some of the products and other things you produce from your land. There are many things that you can make from products from your homestead that will help generate an income. It is not just about selling vegetables at the local farmers market.

You can certainly sell produce at a farmers market, but you can also sell directly from your homestead, or through a local CSA. This is not just limited to fruits and vegetables either. If you can grow high-quality flowers, you can also partner with local flower shops and become a supplier for them.

If you enjoy sharing your homesteading knowledge with others, you can teach in-person or virtual classes about homesteading. This can be anything from foraging for mushrooms, beekeeping, food preservation, or general gardening tips. One of the best things about teaching an online class is that you can create the class once and then continually make passive income from it.

If you enjoy working online, writing, or creating videos then you can start a blog, YouTube channel, or freelance your writing services. Many homesteaders have been able to replace their full-time income doing one of these activities while having the ability to share their knowledge and experience of homesteading.

Another common way that homesteaders earn an income is through making and selling homemade crafts or gifts. You can partner with local artisan stores to sell your products or set up shop at craft fairs.

You can also earn an income from your livestock by either selling the animals for breeding or by selling the products and byproducts of your animals, such as grass-fed meats. There are also many different specialty products that you can sell, like mushrooms and foraged goods. Make a plan to develop both passive and multiple streams of income; the more the merrier!

FINAL WORDS

WHILE HOMESTEADING IS a very big commitment and can be quite an investment to get started, it can also be hugely rewarding. Being able to grow food from seeds, work in your garden, harvest and prepare your own crops, is an incredibly rewarding experience. This, in my mind, is what homesteading is all about: self-sufficiency.

From my time as a homesteader and living off the grid, I have met with many other people in the same lifestyle. While homesteaders and those that live off-grid have varying degrees of self-sufficiency, one of the things that they all have in common is the desire to live off of and give back to the land.

Many people living in rural areas are simply taking from the land and continually consuming. This is a very big draw for those that want to start their own homesteads. They want the ability to do things on their own terms and be producers rather than consumers. Being able to produce food for yourself, your family, and those around you is a very rewarding experience.

Not only are you producing food for others, you are also directly giving back to the Earth. Particularly, when you incorporate things like composting and using organic fertilizers made from byproducts produced on your homestead, it turns into this beautiful symbiotic relationship of give and take.

Every day, people are realizing that the way we are currently living in cities and crowded societies, is not going to be able to sustain the human race long-term. Most modern food production methods are not only making humans sicker but also making the Earth sicker. Turning to homesteading is our way of contributing back to the Earth. Not to mention, the views from your homestead are much better than anything you will ever see in the middle of a city.

Like all good things, starting your homestead is not going to happen overnight. There is a lot that you need to learn and you have to know for certain that it's the right thing for you to do. Homesteading is not something that you can just dabble in, other than trying your hand at small container gardening first.

It is my hope that this book has given you the knowledge you need in order to successfully start and run your homestead. I also hope that if you weren't already convinced in the first place, this book has given you some insight into why homesteading is such a great option.

Jumping right into homesteading, unprepared and without a plan, will likely only end in disaster. You have to make sure that you have done your research, especially for your particular area, when it comes to things like laws, regulations, and hardiness zones. Whether you plan everything out using a notebook and pencil or some type of computer software, just make sure that you have all of your ducks in a row (pun intended) before you make the leap.

Even if you do not consider yourself as having a green thumb, and you have never actually successfully grown anything in your life, it is my hope that this book has given you the confidence to pick up your trowel and start digging.

So, stop putting it off, saying that it will happen someday. Making excuses as to why you cannot start your homestead is not going to get you any closer to your goals of self-sufficiency.

Now before I end this book, I would like to do a quick exercise with you.

I want you to visualize what your homestead is going to look like. Then, I want you to visualize how you are going to feel when you have created your perfect homestead.

This is something that I use to do years ago before I was a homesteader. I would visualize what my homestead looked like, picturing the various crops I would grow, the various animals I would raise, and my big beautiful antique tractor. Then, after I had the image of this perfect homestead in my mind, I would focus my efforts on how I actually felt.

I know, I know.

Visualization is not for everyone, but you should give it a chance.

Visualizing your goals can help you put parameters on them and look at them as if they are actually happening. This helps give you the extra drive that you need to work toward achieving your goals.

So, do this in the morning when you first get up or do it as you are commuting to your job in the city. The important thing is that you truly visualize what your ideal life looks like on your ideal homestead and how you will ideally feel.

Then take those feelings and visualizations and put them into action. Oftentimes, people can set their goals and then work backwards from there. The key point I am trying to make is that it is going to take a lot of hard work to build your homestead. You need to be physically and mentally prepared in order for it not to feel like a burden, which is definitely not the goal here.

The goal is your beautiful homestead which you work hard at every day.

RESOURCES

Agricultural Study Blog. (2019, February 25). Difference between Hot Bed & Cold Frame. Retrieved September 18, 2019, from http://cststudy. blogspot.com/2019/02/difference-between-hot-bed-cold-frame.html

Arbor Day Foundation. (2019). Tree Care Tips & Techniques at arborday.org. Retrieved September 18, 2019, from https://www.arborday.org/trees/tips/

Baessler, L. (2018, April 4). City Gardens In Shade - How To Grow An Urban Garden With Little Light. Retrieved September 19, 2019, from https://www. gardeningknowhow.com/special/urban/urban-gardening-in-low-light.htm

Better Homes and Gardens. (2019). How to Use Hardiness Zone Information. Retrieved September 15, 2019, from https://www. bhg.com/gardening/gardening-by-region/how-to-use-hardiness-zone-information/

Bradbury, K. (2009, December 5). Storing and

Preserving Your Garden Harvest. Retrieved September 17, 2019, from https://www.growveg.com/guides/storing-and-preserving-your-garden-harvest/

Bonnie Plants. (2019). The Basics of Fertilizing – Bonnie Plants. Retrieved September 18, 2019, from https://bonnieplants.com/gardening/the-basics-of-fertilizing/

Botanical Online. (2019, September 16). Fruit trees characteristics. Retrieved September 19, 2019, from https://www.botanical-online.com/en/botany/fruit-trees

Boris, J. (2016, March 23). Blain's Farm & Fleet | Great Brands, Great Value. Retrieved September 17, 2019, from https://www.farmandfleet.com/blog/hot-pack-canning-vs-cold-pack-canning/

Boughton. (2019, August 12). Soil Types - Boughton. Retrieved September 4, 2019, from https://www.boughton.co.uk/products/topsoils/soil-types/

BudBurst. (2016, January 1). About Phenology | Budburst. Retrieved September 3, 2019, from https://budburst.org/phenology-defined

Centers for Disease Control and Prevention. (2019, June 6). Prevent Botulism. Retrieved September 17, 2019, from https://www.cdc.gov/botulism/consumer.html

Cool Galapagos. (2019). Plant groups - the

classification of plants. Retrieved September 18, 2019, from https://www.coolgalapagos.com/biology/classification_plants.php

Coyle, APD, D. (2019, January 15). What Is Fermentation? The Lowdown on Fermented Foods. Retrieved September 16, 2019, from https://www.healthline.com/nutrition/fermentation

Crank, R. (2019, June 17). 5 Homestead Animals for Self-Sufficiency - Countryside. Retrieved September 17, 2019, from https://iamcountryside.com/homesteading/5-homestead-animals-for-self-sufficiency/

Dore, J. (2008). Green Manures – the Good, the Bad and the Ugly. Retrieved September 14, 2019, from https://www.growveg.com/guides/green-manures-the-good-the-bad-and-the-ugly/

Farmer, A. (2018, April 3). Organic Fertilizers. Retrieved September 6, 2019, from https://farmhomestead.com/organic-fertilizers/

Flanders, D. (2019). The Proper Way to Water Your Garden. Retrieved September 17, 2019, from https://www.hgtv.com/outdoors/gardens/planting-and-maintenance/the-proper-way-to-water-your-garden

Fresh Preserving. (2019). Water Bath Canning: Simple Steps for High Acid Foods| Ball®. Retrieved

September 15, 2019, from https://www.freshpre-serving.com/waterbath-canning.html

Fresh Preserving. (2018). Pressure Canning: High Temperatures for Low Acid Foods | Ball®. Retrieved September 15, 2019, from https://www.freshpre-serving.com/pressure-canning.html

Folnovic, T. (2019). Importance of Weather Monitoring in Farm Production. Retrieved September 18, 2019, from https://blog.agrivi.com/post/impor-tance-of-weather-monitoring-in-farm-production

Gendel, W. (2013, December 30). FOOD DEHYDRATION & ENZYMES. Retrieved September 17, 2019, from https://foreverhealthy.net/resources/articles/food-dehydration-enzymes/

Good Housekeeping. (2018, June 27). How to Mulch Your Garden and Stop Weeds in Their Tracks. Retrieved September 18, 2019, from https://www.goodhousekeeping.com/home/gardening/a20706549/how-to-mulch-your-garden/

Grow Great Plants. (2017, January 16). Light, Medium and Heavy Feeders. Retrieved September 18, 2019, from http://www.growgreatvegetables.com/fertilizers/fertilizer-needs-of-vegetables/

Grow It Organically. (2019). Composting Basics, How Does Composting Work, Composting Instructions. Retrieved September 14, 2019, from https://www.grow-it-organically.com/compost-ing-basics.html

Grow Veg. (2013, June 1). Planning Irrigation for your Garden [YouTube]. Retrieved September 14, 2019, from https://www.youtube.com/watch?v=e31dixwSXOk

Grunert, J. (2019). Plant Growth Factors. Retrieved September 15, 2019, from https://garden.lovetoknow.com/garden-basics/plant-growth-factors

Heideri, I. (2017, January 19). How many pounds of meat can you get from an average steer? - Quora. Retrieved September 17, 2019, from https://www.quora.com/How-many-pounds-of-meat-can-you-get-from-a-average-steer

Huang, D. (2019, May 4). 10 VEGETABLES YOU CAN REGROW FROM SCRAP. Retrieved September 19, 2019, from https://about.spud.com/blog-regrowing-vegetables-from-scrap/

Iannotti, M. (2019, June 1). What Is Succession Planting? Retrieved September 14, 2019, from https://www.thespruce.com/succession-planting-1403366

Jakob, A. (2019, January 15). Gardening Where it is Cold (Zone 3). Retrieved September 16, 2019, from https://northernhomestead.com/gardening-where-it-is-cold/

Jenna, J. (2014, April 29). How To Butcher A

Chicken. Retrieved September 17, 2019, from https://theelliotthomestead.com/2014/09/how-to-butcher-a-chicken/

Johnny's Selected Seeds. (2018). Succession Planting Interval Chart for Vegetables | Johnny's Selected Seeds. Retrieved September 14, 2019, from https://www.johnnyseeds.com/growers-library/vegetables/succession-planting-interval-chart-vegetables.html

Karuga, J. (2016, April 1). What Is A "Furrow" (in Agriculture)? Retrieved September 14, 2019, from https://www.worldatlas.com/articles/what-is-a-furrow-agriculture.html

Kirsten, J. (2019, May 19). Types of Plants | 4 Major Classifications of Plants | BioExplorer. Retrieved September 18, 2019, from https://www.bioexplorer.net/types-of-plants.html/

Kurtz, L. (2019, September 6). Apply Mulch. Retrieved September 14, 2019, from https://www.wikihow.com/Apply-Mulch

Lehigh County Master Gardeners. (2019, September 15). Cool-season vs. Warm-season Vegetables. Retrieved September 19, 2019, from https://extension.psu.edu/cool-season-vs-warm-season-vegetables

Live Science. (2012, June 12). What's the Difference Between a Fruit and a Vegetable? Retrieved

September 18, 2019, from https://www.livescience.com/33991-difference-fruits-vegetables.html

MacKenzie, J., & Grabowski, M. (2018). Saving vegetable seeds | UMN Extension. Retrieved September 17, 2019, from https://extension.umn.edu/planting-and-growing-guides/saving-vegetable-seeds

Mantis. (2018, June 6). Cultivating the Soil: Why it's Important and How it Differs from Tilling. Retrieved September 14, 2019, from https://mantis.com/cultivating-the-soil-why-its-important-and-how-it-differs-from-tilling/

Martens Forney, J. (2019). Staggered Planting: What It Is and Why You Should Be Doing It. Retrieved September 6, 2019, from https://www.hgtv.com/outdoors/gardens/planting-and-maintenance/discover-staggered-planting

Morgan, L. (2016, September 1). The Full Menu: Beneficial Elements for Plant Growth. Retrieved September 15, 2019, from https://www.maximum-yield.com/the-full-menu/2/977

Morning Chores. (2019a, August 4). 31 Important Things You Should Do This Fall (Before Winter) on Your Homestead. Retrieved September 18, 2019, from https://morningchores.com/homestead-fall/

Morning Chores. (2019b, August 18). 16 Reasons Beekeeping is Awesome (and Why You Should Do it

Too!). Retrieved September 17, 2019, from https://morningchores.com/why-beekeeping/

Morning Chores. (2019c, August 20). 6 Best Farm Animals to Raise (and 1 Not to) When You're Just Starting out. Retrieved September 17, 2019, from https://morningchores.com/best-farm-animals/

NMSUaces. (2009, November 6). How To Prepare Garden Soil For Planting [YouTube]. Retrieved September 14, 2019, from https://www.youtube.com/watch?v=6RAqGyV6TZo

Nuata, P. (2012). Companion Planting Chart – Garden With Companion Plants. Retrieved September 14, 2019, from https://www.smiling-gardener.com/organic-vegetable-gardening/companion-planting-chart/

Pennington. (2019, January 23). Why and How to Use Soil Amendments. Retrieved September 4, 2019, from https://www.pennington.com/all-products/fertilizer/resources/the-gardeners-guide-to-soil-amendments

Planet Natural. (2019a, July 4). Harvesting and Preserving the Garden | Planet Natural. Retrieved September 17, 2019, from https://www.planetnatural.com/organic-gardening-guru/garden-harvest/

Plant Natural. (2019b, May 17). Anthracnose Disease: Symptoms, Treatment and Control | Planet Natural. Retrieved September 18, 2019, from https://www.planetnatural.com/pest-problem-solver/plant-disease/anthracnose/

Plant Care Today. (2019a, August 31). Making Compost Tea: What Is It and How Do You Use It? Retrieved September 18, 2019, from https://plant-caretoday.com/compost-tea.html

Plant Care Today. (2019b, September 16). 10 Natural Homemade Organic Fertilizer Recipes. Retrieved September 18, 2019, from https://plantcaretoday.com/natural-organic-fertilizer-recipes.html

Reich, L. (2019, February 7). Soil Testing Is Worth the Effort - FineGardening. Retrieved September 4, 2019, from https://www.finegardening.com/article/soil-testing-is-worth-the-effort

Ritz, J. (2019, January 14). 25 Ways to Use Beeswax. Retrieved September 17, 2019, from https://thepal-eomama.com/2015/11/18/25-ways-to-use-beeswax/

Rise and Shine Rabbitry. (2014, May 4). NOSE TO TAIL-Uses For Every Part Of The Domestic Rabbit. Retrieved September 17, 2019, from https://riseand-shinerabbitry.com/2012/02/11/nose-to-tail-uses-for-every-part-of-the-domestic-rabbit/

Saelinger, T. (2015, October 14). Is grass-fed beef worth the cost? New company wants to deliver it to your door. Retrieved September 17, 2019, from https://www.today.com/food/grass-fed-beef-worth-cost-new-company-wants-deliver-it

SF Gate. (2019, June 5). What Is Row Planting? Retrieved September 14, 2019, from https://homeguides.sfgate.com/what-is-row-planting-13428343.html

SF Gate. (2016, October 7). What Types of Bushes Grow Fruit? Retrieved September 19, 2019, from https://homeguides.sfgate.com/types-bushes-grow-fruit-58271.html

 SF Gate. (2017, November 21). Fruit-Bearing Shrubs. Retrieved September 19, 2019, from https://homeguides.sfgate.com/fruitbearing-shrubs-56366.html

Southern Living. (2019). https://www.southern-living.com. Retrieved September 18, 2019, from https://www.southernliving.com/food/entertaining/edible-flowers

Study.com. (2018). What is Soil? - Definition, Structure & Types - Video & Lesson Transcript | Study.com. Retrieved September 4, 2019, from https://study.com/academy/lesson/what-is-soil-defini-tion-structure-types.html

Spices Inc. . (1970, August 22). The Difference Between Pickling and Fermenting. Retrieved September 17, 2019, from https://www.spicesinc.com/p-8828-the-difference-between-pickling-and-fer-menting.aspx

The Grass-Fed Homestead. (2016, July 24). 5 Reasons

to Consider Sheep for Your Homestead. Retrieved September 17, 2019, from https://www.youtube.com/watch?v=yLgvtTQPJTY

The Inspired Prairie. (2019, August 20). 21 Ways To Plan Your Homestead Correctly | Our 5 Acre Journey. Retrieved September 15, 2019, from https://www.theinspiredprairie.com/5-acre-land-layout/

The Tiny Life. (2018, May 7). The Basics of Homestead Gardens (For Non-Gardeners) | The Tiny Life. Retrieved September 18, 2019, from https://thetinylife.com/basic-tips-for-homestead-gardens/

The Spruce. (2019, July 1). 10 Awesome Veggies to Grow in Containers. Retrieved September 6, 2019, from https://www.thespruce.com/great-vegetables-to-grow-in-containers-848214

Tollefsen, R. (2019). Consider Zoning Laws when Purchasing Homestead Land û Homesteading and Livestock û MOTHER EARTH NEWS. Retrieved September 14, 2019, from https://www.motherearthnews.com/green-homes/consider-zoning-laws-purchasing-homestead-land-zbcz1907

Tower Garden . (2019). Fresh Is Best: When (and How) to Harvest Your Own Healthy Produce. Retrieved September 18, 2019, from https://www.towergarden.com/blog.read.html/en/2017/6/harvesting.html

Wauters, B. (1982). File a Declaration of

Homestead | MOTHER EARTH NEWS. Retrieved September 14, 2019, from https://www.motherearthnews.com/homesteading-and-livestock/declaration-of-homestead-zmaz82jazgoe

Wolfe, D., & Wolfe, M. (2019). Vegetables You Can Grow in Two Months or Less. Retrieved September 19, 2019, from https://www.foodnetwork.com

Zerbe, L. (2018, August 9). Why You Should Stop Pruning Your Garden in the Fall. Retrieved September 18, 2019, from https://www.goodhousekeeping.com/home/gardening/a20705769/why-you-should-stop-pruning-your-trees-in-the-fall/